THE
RESTORING
WORD

Preaching as Pastoral Communication

J. Randall Nichols

1817

Harper & Row, Publishers, San Francisco

Cambridge, Hagerstown, New York, Philadelphia, Washington,
London, Mexico City, Sao Paulo, Singapore, Sydney

Portions of Chapter 7 of this work originally appeared in *Theology Today*.

FIRST EDITION

Library of Congress Cataloging-in-Publication Data

Nichols, J. Randall.
  The restoring word.

  Bibliography: p.
  Includes index.
  1. Preaching. 2. Communication (Theology)
I. Title.
BV4211.2.N49 1987   251   86-45821
ISBN 0-06-066111-9

87 88 89 90 91 HC 10 9 8 7 6 5 4 3 2 1

To Robert E. Buxbaum, friend and brother of my
journey, who finally got a footnote

Christ be with me, Christ within me,
Christ behind me, Christ before me,
Christ beside me, Christ to win me,
Christ to comfort and restore me,
Christ beneath me, Christ above me,
Christ in quiet, Christ in danger,
Christ in hearts of all that love me,
Christ in mouth of friend and stranger.

Irish Hymn
"The Breastplate of St. Patrick"

Contents

77065

Preface

I have chosen to write directly and somewhat personally to ministers and seminarians in this book, and so perhaps a personal word about the writing is appropriate as a preface. When I read a book, I am always curious about what it was like for the author to have written it. Was it a labor of love, a trial by fire, just ploughing the back forty one more time? Where is the connecting link between idea and person, between knowledge and history, that brings a book to completion?

Unlike my earlier *Building the Word: The Dynamics of Communication and Preaching,* which virtually wrote itself in a short time one summer, this one was a longer labor and a more difficult delivery. It represents my attempt to combine two aspects of my professional ministry that I do not always get a chance to fit together: teaching preaching and practicing psychotherapy. I have made a strong internal connection between them for years but had never before set myself the task of writing about it directly. The difficulty in doing it was knowing where to start or stop, since there is very little written on the subject of pastoral communication and the field still must be considered wide open, I believe. Besides, I had a few bones to pick with what *was* being said (as is my style, evidently) and needed to work as hard as I could toward being a gentleman about it.

I also discovered that writing a book and ending a long marriage at the same time are not the easiest combination of things, though my hope is that the painfulness of the latter has focused some of my sensitivity for the subject. God knows I needed to hear the kind of preaching I am trying to teach here—but mostly I did not get it. Again and again, though, the existential reality of what I was trying to say hit me hard: we are all in need of restoration, some of us more desperately than others, and for the preacher not to use himself or herself pastorally in the proclamation of the word only impoverishes both our ministry and the healing richness of the gospel.

I must say a little here about several people who were more important to this writing than they knew. One of the joys I anticipated was showing the manuscript to my friend and former mentor Seward Hiltner. His death before it was finished took that away, compounding the loss for me. He had been looking forward to seeing it, and I badly wanted his keenly candid but always loving reaction, knowing in advance that he would never, ever condone my use of the terms *therapy* or *therapist* when, in his view, *counsel* was quite enough.

Obviously the many students, counseling clients, parishioners, and friends who have taught me by their experience must remain anonymous here in the interest of confidentiality, but they have my unreserved thanks for doing what I often believe is the hardest of all things: sharing parts of our brokenness with another human being.

Then there are some people very dear to me who, as things have gone, need to remain wraithlike here, though I would give nearly anything that it had not turned out so. They taught me to love again and even to be able to laugh a little, as when putting the final touches on the manuscript I realized this had been a three-woman book, so to speak. I had wanted to share more of the writing of it with them, but it was not to be. The ending sermon, "The City of Sadness," first preached one stinking hot July Sunday in 1983 with sweat-soaked handkerchief in hand (and perhaps some other moisture as well), is a tribute to some of that.

The next project beckons, but I give you *The Restoring Word* with fear and trepidation, on the one hand, and thanks to God for your comradeship, on the other.

J. Randall Nichols

Introduction

A young woman in my congregation once explained to me why she so seldom came to worship. I knew that she had more than her share of personal troubles, though combined with a tenacity that kept her going when many of the rest of us would have dropped out of the race. What she said, though, threw me and has stayed with me ever since: "I don't come to church much because I'm afraid I will cry, and I know you're not supposed to do that in church." No amount of persuasion from me or anyone else could undo what she had so thoroughly learned—that personal vulnerability and "coming to church" do not mix. Knowing the kind of church life the woman had been raised in and, prominent in it, the preaching she had heard, I was not really surprised, no matter how heartbroken, to hear it.

Books about preaching do not usually have dramatic beginnings, and I do not mean that vignette to be one. But as much as anything else I can recall it symbolizes the reason behind this book and what I hope to do with it. In the last generation we have made some remarkable advances in pastoral care and in our understanding, on both psychological and theological grounds, of how the human drama unfolds. We can now expect currently trained ministers to have both an understanding of and a sympathy for the complex workings of human relationship, feeling, and development. Ministers are not, by and large, "therapists," but increasingly they bring to their work a comprehension of the interplay between theological and psychological dynamics that makes them first-line members of what we loosely (and perhaps too shyly) call the "helping professions." Preaching, too, has made great strides, surviving the decline of the great "royal" pulpits and even, I am convinced, surpassing earlier eras in insightfulness and skill. The trouble is that those two trends have not often enough intersected, either in theory or in practice. Preaching and pastoral care remain different realms of ministry, and most ministers I have ever met struggle to one degree or another to integrate what their instincts tell them *ought* to be dimensions of a single greater unity, even while their practice perpetuates a troublesome vocational and theological split.

Sometimes it can be really bad. I have heard ministers say things in pulpits that they would never dream of uttering in a pastoral conversation, and all too often they are unaware of the contradiction. And I have seen ministers in pastoral settings virtually paralyzed because what they thought they had been taught about preaching and about pastoral principles seemed so irreconcilable that the only conscionable recourse was either silence or triviality. Somewhere between those extremes, however, most of us wrestle with some uneasy combinations of commitment and practice, hoping for a way to bind them together with consistency and integrity.

We struggle with the roles of pastor and preacher, which do not fit easily together nearly as often as we would like to think. The pastor is a tolerant listener, committed to meeting people "where they are" and serving them by presence and shared experience. The preacher, by contrast, is a talker, a representative of the imperatives of the gospel and its claim on human life, an advocate for change and self-transcendence. How can one person consistently do both?

We struggle with the human needs we are called to serve, trying to meet them in our pastoral work but then realizing in our proclamatory roles that often the gospel *defines* and *challenges* needs rather than meeting them. What do we do when the hopes and efforts of people who come to us for help are misdirected, as Christian faith would see it, yet in the agony of the moment no humane way of addressing that divergence appears?

We struggle with different language systems, psychological and theological, which despite the heroic efforts of such pioneers in integrative thinking as Seward Hiltner or Paul Pruyser, are still largely separate linguistic worlds. Often as not we simply become bilingual, talking the sometimes highly technical language of the human experience as pastors but switching to God-talk when we change into our pulpit gowns.

We struggle with the us-and-them dilemma, wondering in a given moment whether to bind up our people's wounds or send them out into the world for service, not so different sometimes from the battlefield physician's painful choice between moving a soldier to safe recovery and patching him up for further fighting. Worship services typically cannot quite make up their minds whether the point of the experience is inside or outside the sanctuary walls.

We struggle with the related but not always congruent ministries of interpretation, on the one hand, and information giving, on the other. Is our task to help people make sense of their lives, using whatever raw material they bring by way of prior experience and understanding? Or is it to give them more information about the gospel and so, perhaps, to change them? Where is the balance between helping people *make* meaning for themselves and *telling* them, on perfectly unassailable grounds, what we believe is true?

Those are not simple choices; they are the continuing tensions that define our professional lives as pastors and preachers. No vote can be taken, no "right" answer found. Any minister who "decides" that in a given moment the correct path lies with either the pastoral or the prophetic side is fated to be wrong; yet the way we go about our pastoral and our preaching work too often seems to cross its fingers and hope that, for the moment, at least, the struggle has gone back into its cave and we can proceed unhindered. Though the word *dialectic* may be new to them, working ministers typically function day in and day out in the midst of dialectical tension between such polarities as these. What is it that holds them together, binds them up, gives us enough altitude to see unities without denying differences, resolves the conflict of our daily work?

There are no easy answers, of course, but there *is* a metaphor that may guide our thinking and perhaps lead us to some new perceptions. It is the familiar—but, I believe, undervalued— idea of *restoration*. Here is one of those concepts (or symbols, if you prefer) that, when looked at long and carefully enough, displays an unsuspected inner dynamism, a little like a gyro that looks perfectly steady from the outside but is a whirling balance of forces within. *Restoration* carries a dual commitment to past and future, old and new, here and elsewhere. It refuses to allow a simple vote between its opposing forces, choosing instead to hold them together in such a way that we slowly come to a different level of thinking altogether.

Central to this book is the conviction that *restoration* is the task of ministry and that from such a perspective some of those painful dichotomies can become creative tensions instead of crippling dilemmas. The work of restoration is neither losing the past nor living in it but rather creating a *present* that reaches realistically out to both past and future. Restoration is neither harsh confrontation of the inadequacies of what and whom we deal with nor passive acceptance of them; it involves the creation of something new that both acknowledges its ancestry and embraces the growing yet to come.

Here I have to do what I usually do when thinking about a complex and abstract subject, and that is to rest a moment in the earthy imagery that either gave it birth or offers to redeem it, I am not sure which. I am a gardener of sorts, and I have the yet-unfulfilled dream of one day restoring a fine old garden. *New* gardens I have built aplenty, and I have reaped the special joy of seeing bare lots or tangled patches of woodland become places of beauty and abundance. But one day I hope to come upon a garden, once ordered and lovely, now gone to rack and ruin and crying out for, well, *restoration*.

It will have to be a careful project. The basic outlines of the garden will have to be discovered among the weeds and encroaching sod. Those plantings that have outlasted even the overgrowth that covers them will have to be protected from an overzealous hoe. I will have to do my horticultural homework to discover what was growing when and whether it is worth preserving. I will have to discipline myself to respect the integrity of this garden as it was and not try to make it something it could never possibly have been. At the same time, I will have to be ruthless with its enemies, giving it the protection it lacked for so long and inviting its dormant strength to rise and do for itself what I, with my techniques and tools, can never duplicate. To *restore* this place of magic and beauty I will have to learn to think very differently about who I am to it, what it needs, what its function was and will be. In it, sweaty, hopeful, shuffling through compost, I can be neither priest nor prophet, in the old sense. My vocation is not really either to pluck up or to plant but to *restore*.

That is how I think of the relationship of pastoral care and preaching. It is what I want to invite you to in these pages, filled as they are with unanswered questions and unsolvable problems, so that, whatever else we say, the word we speak on God's or our people's behalf may be a restoring one.

The subject is shot through with an unsolved and probably unsolvable mystery: *How can a word restore?* What is it about speaking that makes it so potent in the human experience? We all know for a fact that it is. Here and there in even the most dismal human drama, words can release the most exquisite pleasure, can shift our perception to unthought-of possibility, can so impact our lives that we are never quite the same. Yet we also know that words can maim the human spirit, tear out tender shoots of hope, tip us over into bottomless sorrow. How do they do it?

This book cannot answer that question any more than a horticultural guide can tell me by what inner mystery the garden flourishes again after all my efforts. But it can provide an opportunity for some careful watching of the restorative process at work, and from so doing perhaps we can become more careful stewards of these words we are so immersed in. That is my aim.

This rather personal interlude is probably the closest I will come to writing about the glue that holds this whole book together. I want you to think what it is like to sit in worship, hearing a sermon (along with many other things, not unrelated despite our carelessness or sometimes our intention) and gathering whatever resources you have to return to wherever you came from.

As I look out over the landscape of my discipline—"homiletics" in the old lexicon, "theology and communication" in the new—what grieves me most is the almost total lack of attention we have given to the simple question What is it like to hear? With students and, I am afraid, with working preachers, too, that question almost never gets asked. I do not mean we are insensitive to the needs of our people or careless about trying to speak to them. What worries me is that we seem not to know how to ask the question. Robert Lindner, a psychoanalyst known to many of you not so much by his name as by his popular 1950s study *Rebel Without a Cause,* has also written a moving account of treating a schizophrenic physicist who was convinced that much of his time was spent in another galaxy and civilization. Lindner treated the man in the only way that held any promise of a cure, despite the real dangers to the therapist himself: he decided to enter that crazy world and simply inhabit it for a while, in hopes of slowly leading his patient out again. The risk, of course, was that *neither* of them would find the exit.

The case is intricate, beautiful, and frightening. At the end two things stand out for me. One is Lindner's own confession that what he had to do was risk becoming slightly mad himself in order to join and perhaps reclaim the tortured mind of his patient. He writes of the closing days of therapy, of playing out the whole insane drama he had scripted himself into, complete with maps and charts of this extragalactic world. He speaks of his real (not forced) enthusiasm for his weekly journeys to it and then of slowly realizing that the energy for these voyages was coming now not so much from his patient as from himself.

One day the patient balked at leaving planet Earth for his mad refuge and carefully, lovingly, we may imagine, told his doctor, "It's been weeks since I gave up that foolishness." "Then why," the doctor asked, "did you pretend? Why did you keep on telling me—?" "Because I had to," the patient said. "Because I felt you wanted me to."[1]

To restore something means I have to enter it, and there is always the risk that my footsteps will be too clumsy, trampling the very thing I aim to help. But in no other way can I really learn what I am aiming for. Only when I know enough to ask, "What is it like to hear?" do I stand a chance of knowing how to speak restoratively.

The other thing that strikes me is Lindner's own reflection, years later, on that perilous journey and its near disaster:

Until Kirk Allen came into my life I had never doubted my own stability. The aberrations of mind, so I had always thought, were for others. Tolerant, somewhat amused, indulgent, I held to the myth of my own mental impregnability. Superior in the knowledge that I, at least, was completely sane and could not—no matter what—be shaken from my sanity, I tended to regard the foibles of my fellows, their fears, their perplexities, with what I know now to have been contempt.

I am shamed by this smugness. But now, as I listen from my chair behind the couch, I know better. I know that my chair and the couch are separated only by a thin line. I know that it is, after all, but a happier combination of accidents that determines, finally, who shall lie on that couch, and who shall sit behind it.

It has been years since I saw Kirk Allen, but I think of him often, and of the days when we roved the galaxies together. Especially do I recall Kirk on summer nights on Long Island, when the sky over Peconic Bay is bright with quivering stars. And sometimes, as I gaze above, I smile to myself and whisper: "How goes it with the Crystopeds? How are things in Seraneb?"[2]

"How are things?" That is what I want us to learn to ask. Not, for a change, to be too engulfed in our own anxiety to do the preaching job well, to "be faithful" even, or to pass muster at whatever theological way station we have stopped into on the journeys of our ministry; but just to wonder what it is like for our listeners to be sitting there with whatever part of the world has been planted on their shoulders, hearing, striving, or maybe, when it comes right down to it, just barely breathing. To ask that, however, is to do what Lindner did, less dramatically, to be sure, but no less consequentially. As the earliest church sang, "Not counting equality a thing to be grasped, he emptied himself and took the form of a servant (Phil. 2:6–7)." Or an interplanetary traveler—or simply a hearer.

Hardly a more moving description of what it is like to ask that question can be found than this one in an old essay of Karl Barth's:

The impenetrable muteness of the so-called nature that surrounds us, the chance and shadowy existence of every single thing in time, the ill fortune and ill fate of nations and individuals, the basic evil, death—thoughts of these things come to us, disquiet us, and crowd out all that might assure us God is present. The question will no longer down, but breaks out in flame: *is it true?* Is it true, this sense of a unity in diversity, of a stationary pole amid changing appearances, of a righteousness not somewhere behind the stars but within the events which are our present life. . . ? Is it true, this talk of a loving and good God, who is more than one of the friendly idols whose rise is so easy to account for, and whose dominion is so brief? What the people want to find out and thoroughly understand is, *Is it true? So* they come to us, entering into the whole grotesque situation of Sunday morning. . . . They want to find out and thoroughly understand: they do not want to hear mere assertions and asseverations, however frequent and enthusiastic they may be. And they want to find out and thoroughly understand the answer to this one question, *Is it true?*[3]

The point, you see, is that our preaching job is not to tell them what truth is, least of all in the fine theological detail of which we are admittedly often capable, but rather to respond to their question "Is it true?" And that, of course, is what theology *is,* for preaching or anything else. *How* we answer it is fraught with difficulties—no getting around that. But the idea that it is the starting point for pastoral preaching is what I seek to plant here, just because it is one of those things that we all know but do not always remember.

There is an old story, no doubt true but by now often repeated and reascribed, of a young researcher caught up in the complexity and importance of his work, who was one day admonished by his teacher: "Mr. Jones, you must remember that your job is not so much to find out whether X is true as to discover the truth about X." A nice distinction, and perfectly on target for pastoral preaching. Our task is not really telling people that the gospel is true so much as helping them discover the whole truth about their lives. Our commitment is to the idea that life at its "truest" is addressed by the gospel, transformed by it. We believe there is good news there for people who know about their brokenness and helplessness. But there is still that business about answers making no sense until you know the questions, and we often forget this in our zeal to bring relief for some of the pain that is given into our care whenever we preach. Perhaps a physician's help does not always depend on a patient's knowing and believing what a certain medication is going to do before it does it, but preachers are not so lucky.

We can talk all day long about what the gospel does, and people can even nod approvingly at what we say, but until they sense that their brokenness is known and valued, until they themselves can perceive and feel what it is they suffer and need, no connection gets made. There is an analogy to be made here to the physical world. You can swirl certain chemicals together in the same beaker and nothing will happen until you add another ingredient that acts as a catalyst, *allowing* the interaction that was potentially there all along to happen. I can sit and talk forever with a person who aches unbearably from the hurt he or she has experienced but who is unable to do more than suffer silently without movement or relief, and nothing may happen until I say, "How very much that hurts for you," whereupon a connection is made and pain flows forth, perhaps to be healed.

How does it happen that a word restores? Perhaps the catalyst is the sense of being known; perhaps it is the need we all experience to have other people see for us in order for us to realize what our own senses behold; perhaps it is the permission we sometimes need from another person to acknowledge and accept what we dimly know about ourselves. Whatever it is that happens, the point for preaching is that what we have to offer as good news will not be heard until we ourselves can understand what it is like to hear and can communicate, above all, *that* we understand. Perhaps it comes down to a question of whom we think we are working for; though I wish it were not so, I fear we often do get it mixed up. We think our primary allegiance is to a body of theological content or to an institution or procedure instead of to the people God has created and called. Yes, there are those tensions we spoke of earlier that are bound up in the idea of restoration. But so long as we believe, however variously, in an incarnational theology, there is no real *choosing* to be done between working for God and working for the human beings in our care, for in the latter is God known and served.

A simple reminder is in order: God does not need our protection or our care. God is not encumbered or diminished by theological inaccuracy or even neglect. The gospel is not increased by the quantity or volume of our speech about it. The church is neither purified nor augmented by the care we take for its programs or, for that matter, for orthodoxy. The operative agency in all those things is the response of human beings—to themselves, to each other, to God perhaps, to the church. And hearing that response, articulating it on behalf of others, valuing it even when it is dead wrong, letting our own lives be affected by it, addressing it in love and perhaps correction, is probably the thing we teach ministers to do the least well of all their many skills and learnings. This is certainly true when it comes to preaching.

Here is a minor (very minor, some will rightly say) parable of what I am trying to talk about. A messenger was once sent by his king to deliver vital information to a distant city in the kingdom. Since the messenger bore the king's own agency, he was rehearsed over and over to be sure he had the message right and could deliver it without error. At the appointed time, the messenger set out upon his journey of many days. The first day went well, with good speed and few distractions. At the end of it the messenger again rehearsed the information in his care, to keep it fresh and accurate. On the second day the messenger met a lost child who begged to be restored to her family, and, though not without anxiety about the cost of time and concentration, he took the child along a different route to find her home. That night he rehearsed the message with greater difficulty and the beginnings of concern that he might have lost small parts of it. The third day brought the messenger into a village whose well had gone dry, leaving its inhabitants too weak even to send for help. They begged him to take word to the next town, lest they all perish of thirst and disease, and the messenger reluctantly agreed to do so. That night the message was in parts unclear, and his worry increased.

Each day thereafter found the messenger more distracted, more interrupted. People talked to him, beseeched him, clutched at him, and in his decency he responded as best he could. But each evening, when he rehearsed the king's message, it became less accurate, less clear. When he finally reached his destination, he was in agony, for he knew that he could not deliver what he had been sent to say, and he knew, too, that the penalty for his carelessness would be severe. To the governor of the distant town he presented himself and told his tale, reciting in succession the agonies that had distracted him, beating his breast in repentance for letting himself be so misled from his sworn duty as agent of the king, and ending with his confession that he could not now say the vital words he had so carefully rehearsed in the king's presence.

The governor reached out to the by now trembling messenger and bade him rise from where he had fallen in his shame and fear. "You were not the only messenger, my son," he said. "Our king on the day of your departure dispatched yet another servant, unskilled in memory or perception but carrying in written form the same message entrusted to you. You may read what it says." The message was as follows:

My dear Governor:

There is great suffering in the land, but our people's hearts are hardened. I must find someone with eyes to see, a will to respond, and the courage to share the pain that lies about us to act as my vicar. Pray, tell me if you have such a person, and send him to me at all speed, for the time is short and the responsibility heavy.

The messenger looked up in confusion; his understanding grew as the governor said, "Until you came, I had no such person to send, but now it is clear that you are he. Return to the royal service of your king, for you have brought the message ten times over and far more clearly than ever you rehearsed it."

AN AUTOBIOGRAPHICAL NOTE ON TERMINOLOGY

It often seems that the commonest terms in a subject are the most devilishly difficult to pin down. When I had finished the first draft of this book and began to tell people what it was about, I ran smack into that trouble. What did I mean by "therapy" or "pastoral" or "pastoral care"? (Mercifully, no one seemed to have much trouble with "preaching.") I certainly did not want to use half the book defining terms, but obviously some clarification was needed.

The problem was aggravated by my own academic discipline—or lack of it—in theological education, though in the end that provided the key. It is true that I both do and teach preaching, except that in my own institution we call it "theology and communication" in an effort to include more about communication dynamics than the traditional concept of "homiletics" easily allows. But I am also a trained and practicing psychotherapist in the psychoanalytic tradition, which offers yet another language system, slightly different from that of "pastoral theology," which is not my disciplinary background. Somewhere inside me those things were integrated—that was why I was writing this book, after all—but getting to it ("accessing" it, my computer reminds me) was the rub.

I had been thinking for some months, however, about how better to designate my own hybridized "field," and the answer I eventually came up with also seems to solve some of the book's terminological problems. Tying what I do together is a concern for what I shall call *pastoral communication,* leaving open the particular *form* of that communication—preaching, pastoral counseling, educational endeavor, etc. In the secular world this has been called "therapeutic communication," and I intend the more theological term to have much the same force: that aspect of human communication which affects and involves the deeply personal in us and, moreover, which does so to some extent by the design and intention of the communicator. This book, then, would be about *preaching as pastoral communication*. It would not be an effort to integrate preaching and pastoral *care* in the sense of trying to amalgamate two different kinds of ministerial activity. It is specifically the communicative linkage and the pastoral/therapeutic dimension of it that I am talking about.

With that focal point I hope some of the terms become less vexing. When I do speak of "pastoral care" from time to time, you will know that I mean it in the broader sense just mentioned and not as any form of explicit activity such as visitation, counseling, or group leadership. I do retain the terms *therapy* and *therapeutic,* despite the fact that one of my greatest friends and mentors, the late Seward Hiltner, railed all his life against them when they were applied to ministers. Some would make a distinction between *therapy* and *counseling;* in this book I do not, and they are used interchangeably. Even though I hope it is clear that ministers on the whole are not by training or practice "therapists," the force and dynamic of their communication in preaching is often therapeutic, and I think it is both an accurate and a respectable word to use.

The term I am happiest with as an integrating image, however, is "restoration," partly, I suppose, because it moves us well out of the line of fire of sometimes competing disciplines and language systems. It is dominantly the *restorative* power of preaching that I am trying to describe and guide our practice of, and, terminology aside, I believe any minister who has watched someone come alive again because of the power of a word will know what I mean.

1. When Is Preaching Pastoral?

Some would say, of course, that the question "When Is Preaching Pastoral?" is either backward or silly. Isn't *all* preaching "pastoral" in on sense or another? Perhaps in a broad sense, though I do not believe stopping there takes us far enough down the road of understanding what we mean. True enough, most preaching is done by people whom the hearers identify as their pastors, and there are bound to be some connections and resonances even in the most unrelentingly theological discourse or biblical exposition. It is also true enough that all preaching is pastoral if we believe that sound theological thinking and accurate biblical understanding are in service to better personal faith, life, and action (even if that comes a little too close to saying that knowing such things is good for you even if it doesn't seem to matter a whit in terms of any live personal issues you happen to be struggling with!).

We can sharpen things up a great deal, though, by taking the question more seriously and asking what it is that makes or defines or identifies preaching that can be *distinguished* as "pastoral." I am suggesting three answers, that can serve as "definitions" of pastoral preaching. Many of the same issues that will concern us in this book are visible from each of those vantage points, but we need to take some pragmatic differences seriously rather than trying to hammer out one all-purpose point of view.

First, preaching is pastoral in that there is a pastoral *impact* to what is said, regardless of whether it is negative or positive, intended by the preacher or supplied by the hearers. That is as close as we will come to saying that all preaching is pastoral, and it is not at all the same thing. The point is that there is a *dimension* of a sermon that is pastoral even if the overall effort is neither intended nor perceived to be so. This is a functional definition, asking, in effect, "What happened with this communication?" rather than "What kind of message was it?" I imagine, for instance, that a sermon that most of us would say was inherently unconcerned with direct human affairs (perhaps a learned treatise on the significance of the iota subscript in certain theological words used by the Apostle Paul or a meticulous exposition of the role of fire imagery in Old Testament apocalyptic) could be heard and valued as pastorally important by *someone*. Our job on this first definition would then be to take that reception seriously and ask what was involved in it, how even such unlikely material shaped itself as personally meaningful in a particular hearer, and so on. Just as important, we need to take seriously that the *absence* of pastoral concern has a negative pastoral effect insofar as people feel themselves bypassed, unheard, or cheated. We can and should talk about the pastoral dimension of preaching even when a sermon would in no way fit into that category in any kind of homiletical typology. The pastoral impact of a completely intellectualized theological discourse on repentance preached the day after four of the congregation's teenagers were killed by a madman would, to say the least, be profound—even though negative. It will be important for us to keep this first definition in mind when we deal with the communicative value of what is said in preaching rather than with the rhetorical or stylistic or intentional pigeonhole it occupies. Just announcing that a given sermon is "pastoral" does not necessarily make it so, any more than calling it something else forecloses any possible pastoral impact, intended or not.

Second, though, there is preaching that deliberately sets out to touch and involve people's personal concerns, whether on an immediate or a more global level. This is probably the main way preaching is pastoral for most of us most of the time: we try to make it so. For our current purposes let us also say that the *dominant strategy* or perspective of the sermon lies in this realm (taking us a step farther than the first definition). The intent is something more than just a matter of "applying" or "illustrating" the sermon's content in such a way as to graft otherwise relatively impersonal material onto living hearers. The content itself is shaped along a pastoral dimension. So long as we do not try to put too much weight on it, it probably does make sense to think of a typology here in which some sermons are dominantly concerned with pastoral issues, others with biblical interpretation, still others with systematic theological thinking, and so on. Our concern in this definition would be, therefore, with the sermon that sees itself as "pastoral" as opposed to a sermon (perhaps even on the same biblical text, theological topic, or social concern) that would take a very different strategy. (An instructive and revealing discipline for both preachers and congregations is to take a single biblical text that offers sufficient possibilities and develop, say, three different sermons on it from different typological perspectives. That can do a lot to get us unstuck from the outmoded hermeneutical idea that each text has a single "propositional" core meaning that, when found, leads us to the single "right" interpretation.) It is probably more into the realm of this second approach than anywhere that some of the mischief I am going to talk about in these pages creeps unintentionally when, despite our best efforts and sensitivities, what we actually say goes against the grain of the sort of human experience we are trying to cultivate. Here, in other words, is where we wage most explicitly those struggles of which I spoke in the introduction and become most self-conscious about the intersection of the roles of proclaiming the word and shepherding the people. Helping us make better headway in that task is the purpose of this book, and so this second approach to pastoral preaching will be home base.

There is yet a third sense in which we can speak of pastoral preaching, however, and that is the occasion when the very subject of a sermon is itself an issue of pastoral import, whether on an individual or a community scale. When we "preach on" family breakups or depression or a conflict in the congregation or a disaster in the community, we have not only a pastoral *dimension* (the first definition) and a pastoral *strategy* (the second) but also a pastoral *subject* (the third approach). My hope, frankly, is that more of this kind of preaching will be done as ministers are increasingly better attuned to and educated about the inner dynamics of the human experience. I also hope, of course, that you will find yourself freer to tackle this kind of sermon as a result of reading this book, simply because it strikes me as poor homiletical stewardship to let the whole area of mental health and human relationships remain a *tacit* dimension of our preaching—or, still worse, to leave it entirely to such diverse nontheological preaching as the popular psychological press, talk-show interviews, or *Redbook* magazine.

This, then, is what we are going to mean by *pastoral preaching:* the homiletical occasion when, whether by its dimension, its strategy, or its subject, a sermon addresses or impacts the personally invested concerns of its hearers. With that understanding behind us, I think it is safe to use the term *pastoral preaching,* and we will be doing so a lot in the following pages.

Before we begin, however, let me talk a bit less formally and more directly about some of the things at issue here. Despite the care I have tried to take in the preceding lines on "definition," in candid moments I come back to thinking that pastoral preaching is as much as anything a posture, a sensitivity, an attitude. That has to come first, to sharpen our awareness, to guide our crafting, and to give a personally meaningful frame of reference to our work. I have been one of the lucky ones in the mentors I have had, the people I have served, and the opportunities that have come my way. I wish that every preacher could have it that way, and some part of that hope is why I try to write books about it. I wish every preacher could one day receive in the mail a letter such as the following, fictitious in form but as real in content as next week's sermon:

Dear Pastor:

You do not know me yet, but I have visited your worship services several times now. I sit toward the back, am an unremarkable middle-aged person, and act and dress like the reasonably well-put-together human being I am. But listening to your, or anyone's, preaching constitutes a risk of sorts, and I wanted to tell you about some of my fearfulness about that before we go too much further. Since I do not know you, nor you me, and we therefore have no axes to grind, it is a good time to be candid.

I am not always sure why I come to worship, but I have discovered over the years that no matter how routine and habitual the reasons for my getting there, once I sit down something else begins to happen. I have no particular sensitivity for "holy things," but it is clear enough even to me that being in worship means something at least a little out of the ordinary. No one needs to persuade me of that; I am already ready for whatever it will bring, and I want you to know it is a little frightening at times. Since you are obviously in charge of things, I find myself hoping you will, well, be a little careful with me (even though, in truth, I do not break easily).

I hope, for instance, that you will know a little about what it feels like to be in my shoes—or pew, maybe. No, I certainly don't expect you to know my life history—after all, we have never met. What I mean is I want you to know that the aches and struggles I imagine you too have felt (and put aside, as a professional must, when you are up there in the front) are what I sit there holding in my hands. I want you to be on my side, to understand a little of my role. Perhaps it is contradictory, I being a stranger and all, but, you see, I want to feel known and understood. Maybe it is more fair to say I want to feel that you are prepared to offer that understanding, that it is a top priority for you, waiting for whatever chances circumstance might give to make it more concrete.

Then as I wait for you to start talking, I find myself hoping you will be able to help me make sense of what is going on with me. It is almost like going to the doctor for a diagnosis of what is wrong, I guess, though I certainly do not expect you to be a physician or even a mental health expert. But still there is this desire to have someone help me put what I am dealing with, day in and day out, into perspective, to find out what it really amounts to, especially as a Christian believer—though I hope you will not press me too hard to say *exactly* what that means!

Will I be able to sense that your commitment in this service is to me as a person, rather than to something else—your theological thinking or your Bible study, perhaps? I have heard other preachers, I admit, who were nice enough but gave me the impression that the *first* item on the agenda was something besides me as a human being; and for a while there I found myself believing that before anything else I ought to be concerned for believing the right things or backing the right causes. Somehow, it never worked, I suppose because while as a person I could do all that, I somehow couldn't make much headway with any of it *until* I felt my being a person had been taken seriously.

Let's face it; even though I am a fairly tough character and have been around a lot, I sit here wanting you to be gentle with me. I don't mean "coddled," mind you. It's just that sometimes preachers seem so worried that anyone is going to take them seriously they forget how powerful what they say really is. I remember once wondering why my little boy reacted so strongly when I spoke firmly to him, until I listened to myself on a tape recorder and realized just how big and forceful I sounded. No, I'm not talking about your voice, but I want you to know it sometimes doesn't take as much as you might think to get through to me. I'm pretty sensitive about some things, especially the painful ones, and it seems to me they are the ones that get talked about the most when I read the Bible or hear good preaching.

Now, here is a tough one. Sometimes I get frightened at something and pull back into a kind of shell that looks on the outside like self-control or maybe even indifference. The strange thing is that even when that happens I somehow hope you will have the courage and sensitivity to see through it and maybe to talk to me as though it weren't there. I don't mean ignoring it, or battering down my gates, or anything like that. I guess I don't want you to be put off by me; I want you to know that sometimes I'm just protecting myself when I seem to resist what you have to say, and that's when I need you to be braver about it than I am.

Another thing that ministers seem to me to have a hard time with: I want you to take your time with me. You (not you personally, or at least I don't know yet whether this is the case) seem to rush a lot, to feel that everything has to be accomplished right now. Yes, I know there really is a lot of urgent business in the world, but with everyone else around me demanding that things be done yesterday, I come here hoping for a little more patience and a lot more time. If I get it, I'll be back, don't worry.

One last thing, and here I admit I'm out of my territory. But I hope you don't come on sounding like an amateur psychiatrist. What I want, I mean, is what I guess you might call a theological approach. Now, careful here! I don't mean I want you to talk theology instead of talking about me. But it is important to me that my faith gets connected to my life, and I have had all I want of ministers who never quite get around to that. I was told I was "O.K." for so many years I nearly forgot who "I" was sitting in church, if you know what I mean. It just seems to me that a healthy religion fits hand in glove with healthy personhood, and that's what I am hoping to discover more about.

Thank you for listening. I want to hear what you have to say.

Our anonymous letter writer would have done in his or her own way one of the things I hope to accomplish in this book by both reminding us of the person-centeredness of our work and also breaking down some false distinctions that have too often kept preaching and pastoral communication separately conceived and executed. It is common (and basically accurate) to characterize the material of the New Testament as falling into three categories: *kerygma, didache,* and *therapeia.* The first is supposed to be proclamation, the second, teaching or instruction in the Christian life, and the third, the care and nurture of human beings toward the fulfillment of their potentials. Down through the centuries those three concerns, or perspectives, have tended to get themselves institutionalized (and in the process compartmentalized). *Kerygma* became preaching; *didache* turned into Christian education or catechesis; and *therapeia* was the cure of souls or pastoral care. Although there still are useful distinctions to make, those dividing lines have long outlived their usefulness. They do not really refer, least of all in their New Testament sources, to separate ministerial activities so much as to different dimensions of the same ministerial task. They are the strands of a bundled cable, and though one may be more obvious at a given time in a given activity, they are always all there. That is one of the working assumptions of this book, whose special focus is on the way *therapeia* occurs in and through the preaching event.

2. Carefulness in Restoration: The Harm and the Help of Preaching

In *Building the Word* I tried to make the neglected point that preaching, because it is more powerful communication than we sometimes realize, can harm as well as help its consumers.[1] That is, the *worst* preaching can be is not benignly neutral, as we sometimes think. In the pastoral perspective that point becomes even more important, and we need to spend some time with it right at the beginning.

This is not going to be a negative chapter, however, because the overriding concern is what we want pastoral preaching to *do,* what we take as its objectives. As it turns out, "harm" and "help" are two sides of the same coin, in the same way perhaps that the same medication that cures can also make matters worse—sometimes much worse—in the wrong dose or at the wrong time or to the wrong person. The point I will be making again and again in these pages is that *preaching is powerful, far more so than many of us often give it credit for.* To be faithful and responsible to our task we simply have no choice but to find out as best we can both how that power helps and also how, misused, it harms. We need to learn to be as alert and careful with our hearers as we are with the infants we baptize. What we want to do here, then, is to sharpen our goals and, at the same time, to get properly cautious about what can happen when preaching gets off track. I want to talk about nine ways preaching helps or harms, depending on how we go about it.

Bear in mind that when we speak of "preaching" we are almost never talking about a single sermon or even a few but rather about an extended preaching experience. What makes the impact of preaching is far more subtle, for the most part, than the obvious *content* of any one sermon. An apt analogy might be human relationships. What makes the quality of a relationship is not so much any one encounter as rather the accumulation over repeated interactions of almost hidden emphases, styles of thinking, attitudes, expectations, emotional responses, ways of talking or acting, and the like. We could call them *systemic* features of the interaction, meaning that they have to do not so much with what is said or done as with the relational process itself—the glue that holds the pieces together rather than the pieces themselves, perhaps. The same is true for preaching. Week in and week out the preacher communicates not only the topic and thought of the sermon but also those more elusive—and more potent—systemic features that govern how we think about ourselves, other people, God, the world around us, and what the future holds. Those are the things I am talking about now, and by the time we have finished we will have a fairly lengthy list of them.

Just here I must take a deep breath and report something that can be dangerously misunderstood and misapplied but that has to be said anyway: It does not take much in quantity to make a whopping difference in quality when we are talking in the psychological or pastoral dimension. Let me give an example. One of the preaching courses I teach to Master of Divinity students is on the subject of pastoral preaching, and part of the course consists of their writing brief pastoral sermons for critique in class and subsequent revision. After teaching the course for the first time I discovered, far more to my surprise than I am comfortable admitting, that as often as not the amount of revising that needed to be done to these sermons in order to make a very great deal of difference was very small. Changing a sentence or two here and there, adding or deleting a paragraph, altering a repeated phrase or pattern of word choice—such seemingly trifling shifts mattered a great deal. A sermon that went helpfully along lifting up and interpreting certain painful ways that hearers had of coping with life, for instance, would suddenly make an abrupt switch in language style and begin to talk in moral imperatives: lots of "oughts," "shoulds," and "musts," effectively destroying the posture of "interpretative acceptance" the preacher had initially taken. Or a perfectly good sermon on grief in light of Christian faith and hope would just not be able to resist a paragraph about the Resurrection that effectively denied the reality of death, thereby undoing most of what the previous efforts had tried (perhaps successfully) to accomplish. Or a sermon designed to lead hearers into asking tough questions that had no easy answers finished up in confident declaration (both in tone and content) that the way was now clear and the riding easy if only we believed. You begin to see the pattern.

My hesitancy in bringing this up stems from a fear, to put it bluntly, of making preachers more overcautious and obsessional about their preaching than they sometimes already are—which is often quite enough, thank you. The point is that we preachers need two kinds of sensitivity when it comes to pastoral sermons: we need broad, strategic understanding of our objectives and of how, in a dynamic sense, what we say impacts the lives of hearers, but we also need a fine-tuned critical ability to see beneath the surface to the way small details add up to bigger consequences, *particularly when we look at our work as the accumulation of influence over long periods of time.* Whether this is a homiletical variation on Jesus' advice to be wise as serpents and as innocent as doves, I cannot say; but it does have the same paradoxical ring to it, and I want us to keep it in mind.

Let us now turn to nine two-sided coins to talk about the harm and the help of pastoral preaching.

I. DISCOVERING GRACE AND PURPOSE

Frederick Buechner has done as much as any recent theological writer to underline the importance of the "sacred journey" as a metaphor of Christian faith.[2] It is a good image for the first and in some ways most far-reaching purpose of pastoral preaching: *helping people discover God's grace and purpose for their lives.* The operative word here is "discover," for the pilgrimage we are talking about is a process rather than an attachment to a finished program. In both educational and psychotherapeutic circles we know that people learn best and profit most from what they discover for themselves. The role of teacher or therapist is to guide that discovery process, not race ahead to the end and haul people abruptly to the conclusion. The same is true for pastoral preaching. We are inviting people to go searching for grace and purpose. Even when we think we know what they will find, it does little good to tell them: the process more than the outcome is given into our care. Our preaching can be planned and structured accordingly once we have grown sensitive to the difference.

Sometimes, however, the coin comes up tails, and we inadvertently preach in such a way as to close down the search, misdirecting the pilgrims into premature and fickle havens and cheating them—there really is no other word for it—of their sacred journeys. No, we do not *mean* to—of course not. But look at some of the ways the harm is done without our realizing it.

We Work as "Answer People."

Because we undeniably *do* have some information to impart and some confidence we want to instill, we sometimes begin to deal in what I will call (not originally) answer systems, by which I mean that in both style and content we communicate the underlying message "I am a person who has the answers to your questions, and if you listen closely enough I will give them to you." That is perfectly well-meaning, perhaps, but what does it to do that searching and growing we *thought* we were facilitating in people? Again and again as I help my children with their homework I have to bite my lip when I know the answers they are looking for (or think I do), because my role is to guide their discovery process, not deliver an answer system to them. Only then will the answers they eventually get as well as the process by which they got them be really *theirs*.

We Demand to Know the Theological Passwords.

There is a vast difference between teaching people how to use appropriately the language of the Christian tradition and forcing them to comply with a theological code or jargon they do not understand or believe. Because we sound as though *we* know what some of that code means (and sometimes we do), we send the subtle message that they ought also to know already—and, of course, should not be asking about it. The net effect, unhappily, can be to teach people to talk about their lives in theological terms without theological understanding, and again the discovery process is compromised.

We Enforce a Theological "Dress Code."

Just as the word processor on which I am writing uses all kinds of hidden signals that never appear on the printed page but nevertheless tell the electronic gadgetry what to do, so our communication is full of unstated cues that tell people how to "hear." The signal I am thinking of here is overabundant in some preaching: the unstated "of course." "[Of course] God answers the prayers of the faithful." "God walks with us wherever we are [if, of course, we believe]." "The community of faith sustains you in time of confusion [though, of course, you have to come to church]." What is happening here is that we are erecting certain standards for eligibility to be a pilgrim, and in and of itself that is not bad; in fact, it is necessary. The trouble creeps in when we stop being aware of the content of this "dress code" and it becomes unrealistic and restrictive. The message then becomes "You can join our search party only if you play by some rules that have nothing, really, to do with the main objective."

What that amounts to is *forbidding doubt and inquiry,* sometimes by trying to "do theology" apart from the human experience. Our stance becomes entirely deductive ("This is the way it is") rather than inductive ("What do you see and how can we make sense of it?"). I have in mind, for instance, a preacher whose pastoral sensitivity and skill is really quite high but who compensates for his own theological "at-seaness" and uncertainty by becoming heavily theological and dogmatic in his preaching. There is little of the human drama in what he says; not even the divine/human drama of the Bible itself survives the conceptualizing treatment he gives it. Though his words extend what sounds like an invitation to growth and journeying, the total impact of his preaching closes the whole process down. It is one of the most harmful things we can do.

2. LIVING IN THE REAL WORLD

Abram Kardiner, one of the great early psychoanalysts, is supposed to have said once, "The only cure for neurosis is reality." When you think about that for a minute, its absurdly self-evident wisdom makes an impact. Not fancy treatment techniques, not mysterious qualities of the therapeutic relationship, not all the good will or caring in the world, but reality: that is what heals, and the therapist's task is simply (but never easily) to try to lead a person into it. The same can be said for pastoral preaching: one of its major purposes is to help people deal realistically with their lives, even (or perhaps especially) those baffling, conflicted, elusive, and painful parts of living for which *un*realistic ways out are always tempting. As Christians we believe that reality lies in the "what is seen and more," as Ian Ramsey says,[3]—but note the phrase "and more," not "instead of."

There are two strong ways preaching can contribute to a greater sense of reality and competence in living in it. The first is, as you might expect, a direct attention to those issues and forces we have to live with, an attempt to address them in a Christian perspective. Paul's great declaration in 2 Corinthians 4 still stands as one of the greatest affirmations of what it all means to have this treasure in earthenware vessels, to carry within us both death and the life that kills death, to wage our days again and again getting knocked down but not out, as J. B. Philips has it. It is a radically incarnational and sacramental statement: the real creation is *God's,* all of it, and it is at the heart of that reality that the mystery of God's presence lies, even when the heart is breaking.

There is a second dimension, less direct and less talked about, that we should know about and will be coming back to; for now I will just call it the reality of sanctuary. What I refer to is the experience we all have from time to time of discovering that in order to deal with reality we have to in some sense shelter ourselves momentarily from its demands, fall back and regroup, seek a moratorium on the unrelenting pressures of real life. It is a very different thing from running away from it or turning our backs on the world. The ancient image of sanctuary is the best I can think of to describe it, and I would use the same terminology when talking about psychotherapy, in which much the same dynamic occurs.

What happens in therapy is a strange combination of highly intense grappling with reality and at the same time temporary relief from its consequences. In the therapeutic hour a certain distance is achieved from what happens "out there," not so that you can get away from it but rather so that you can look at it more closely *from a safe vantage point*. That is the key: the sanctuary of the therapeutic relationship is what makes it work, a climate in which a client knows that no matter what he or she does or says (given a few basic ground rules like not breaking up the furniture or attacking other people), the listening therapist will not disapprove or run away or censure or seduce. I often tell my own clients that the very artificiality or "unreality" of our once-a-week relationship and situation makes it "more real than real," gives it its leverage for helping people come better to grips with what they must do and how when they return to the street.

The same can be true, I believe, for worship and the preaching that goes on within it. If it goes well, then I am better equipped than before to live out my real life. I grow impatient, I confess, with too-easy criticism about how worship is not enough in touch with live issues of the day and not sufficiently like the marketplace in which we live. That is the point: if it *were* the marketplace instead of a sanctuary, it would lose its unique power to equip me for going back outside and grappling with the reality that is "too much with us" sometimes. The zealous notion that such a retreat into sanctuary weakens or distracts us and ought to be set aside for more direct encounter with the existential pressures of the "world" is, on these terms, nonsense. Just as education is in some sense a "moratorium" from pressures of producing in the social and economic world and psychotherapy is a "holding time" when inner strength is clarified and marshaled, so pastoral preaching presides over a "sanctuary" experience *in service to* (never as substitute for) the exile's return to a broken Jerusalem in need of rebuilding.

That overall goal gets sabotaged in preaching in two primary ways: magical thinking and depersonalization. Though we presumably outgrew our belief in magic in the early years, we probably never get over a certain wistfulness about it. Our harmless little good-luck rituals attest to such a longing, and some of the most enjoyable of our reading (or viewing, I suppose it has to be admitted) taps just that time-tarnished hope that magical solutions will appear for real difficulties. There is a certain charm and spice to it, and I wouldn't give it up or take it away from anyone for the world.

Neither, however, would I want to confuse it with reality, for that way lies, at the extreme, the snakepit of mental illness and, even short of that, the crippling of what makes us human. Fostering magical thinking and solutions, however, is precisely what preaching can do, no matter how inadvertently, when we get careless. Saying that "God will make the pain go away," when everyone with any sense or experience knows it very well may *not,* instead of affirming the presence of God in the very midst of pain is an example. Another is any of several sophisticated translations and variations of that billboard abomination we sometimes still see, "The family that prays together stays together." Not always, and sometimes just as well, sad though it may be. And whoever said that prayer was a magic wand, as

though our doing something in just the right way would cajole
or coerce God's agreement with our self-diagnosis of what is
good for us? Well, I'm afraid that a lot of otherwise well-
intentioned preachers say precisely that, in covert ways, when,
instead of taking as their basic theological message that God
continues to operate in and through his creation as sovereign
Lord even when the going is rough, they picture God as an
otherworldly alternative to what our eyes plainly see and our
hearts indisputably know. It is one thing to say that reality is
grounded in transcendence and shot through with signs of
God's presence; it is something else again to hint that only by
giving up the daily reality we are served will we find relief.

In the same vein, we foster a sense of unreality when we lose
touch with the boundary between words and things, so that the
word in some sense *becomes* the thing, a process called reifica-
tion (or, as I sometimes prefer, "thingification"). I wrote of this
at some length in *Building the Word;*[4] the point here is to remind
us of the pastoral significance of the process: it too contributes
to losing touch with the real world. I was in a board of trustees
meeting recently, for instance, in which we were dealing with a
bookkeeping problem that inadvertently had run us afoul of a
state legal procedure. It was all entirely innocent, but the way
the members' language worked was revealing: we decided to go
on record as not knowing there had been any infraction (which
was entirely true) in hopes of avoiding a monetary penalty. So
far so good. As time went by, however, we began to censor our
conversational language so as not even to allude (in the off-the-
record privacy of the meeting, mind you!) to a possible penalty.
We talked, in other words, *as though* it could not possibly
happen, and the sweet incense of verbal magic began to
perfume the air: as long as we kept the language right, the
reality of having perhaps to pay for our honest mistake would
not exist. That is the sort of thing I mean. (In a more familiar
way, I was doubly saddened at the time to read of Terence
Cardinal Cooke's death in New York: saddened by his dying
and saddened again by the text of the official announcement, to

the effect that he had been "called home." The words of death were never used. How much more *real* it would have been, precisely on theological grounds, to have said, "He died; we believe he was called home to his God.") Christian faith is "what is seen and more"—not "instead of."

Depersonalization is the other way we foster unreality. Here I mean simply ignoring evident personal issues either in the situation we are addressing or, for that matter, in the biblical text that forms the basis of our sermon, if that is the case. Laurence Stookey recently wrote a revealing report on attending a worship service in which, although the sermon itself was on target, the remainder of the service—prayers, hymns, congregational concerns, and so forth—completely blanked out the issues any worshiper would have read about in their local morning paper: rising unemployment, the threat of war, the deaths of people they knew. That was depersonalizing, and its net effect was to subvert the entire purpose of an otherwise good sermon.[5]

In preaching itself depersonalization occurs when we lose touch with the sanctuary dynamics I spoke of earlier and substitute issues for people as the focus of our attention. I am not, of course, saying that *all* preaching has to deal directly with life-determining personal issues (the third of our initial three definitions of pastoral preaching). I do find myself taking the position, though, that as soon as the personal connectedness of preaching is lost, we are in the domain of depersonalization and harm. No, that does not mean that we do not speak with directness and force of the mighty acts of God or the pressures and issues of living in society or the mind-stunning challenges to simple existence offered by a technological world run away from its values or identity. It is the *way* we speak of them that matters, whether we do so in such a way that a listener can "place" himself or herself in them realistically and personally. It is that placement that happens in the sanctuary, and if it has happened well, the world will be different both for us and from us when we return to it.

3. KOINONIA AND COMPETENCE

One of the most marvelous and mysterious things accomplished by the communication *process* itself (leaving aside the content of the message) is the creation of what we sometimes call publics, together with their inner sense of being able to perform in certain ways. People receiving a message together begin to think of themselves as a people-together, a group that shares, at the very least, the common property of being simultaneously involved in this particular communication experience, and more likely a good deal more: a sense of seeing the world in certain ways, of being linked together in common cause, of needing each other or at least of inhabiting the same life-space, for better or worse. They become, in the language of mass communication studies, a public. Moreover, they are a public with a certain competence, an ability to respond to what they are receiving in whatever ways the message itself "instructs" them.

That is how the communication process serves what has long been a goal of preaching and of pastoral preaching in particular: the creation of a community, a *koinonia* that senses itself "called out" for certain purposes. Though our language is mildly different in theological circles, what we are talking about is what the communication analyst would say is what the process indeed does. On top of that, with pastoral preaching we want to be more specific about just what *kind* of community and what kind of purpose we get. We hope to nurture an appropriately *interdependent* community with *competence* to take responsibility for both their own lives and for the "care of the earth" in their keeping. That is the goal.

By interdependent I mean pretty much what we have always understood about bearing one another's burdens (but not shouldering other people's responsibilities), sharing each other's joys and sorrows (though not doing other people's feeling for them), and walking together through the journey of life (but not doing for others what they ought and need to do for themselves). Interdependence is mutuality, openness, common ownership of what matters to us, shared responsibility for what each day brings. There is room in it for both dependence and independence, provided those are woven into the larger fabric and do not become the dominating qualities on their own.

By competence I mean, roughly, the knowledge and ability to do what is appropriate to any of us at any given time—neither shirking responsibility nor trying to climb the north face of the Eiger single-handedly. Competence, that is, is realistic. There is room in it for honest assessment of limitation and for saying "no" when we have to, just as there is room for trying to beat our best record and do what we have never before quite undertaken. As with interdependence, "yes" and "no" are variations on the main theme and neither dominate it nor run from their rightful places.

The harm element appears when our preaching does an about-face and begins to create dependency and helplessness instead of interdependent *koinonia* and competence. It happens, I am afraid, more often and more easily than we would like, again sometimes despite our best intentions.

The relationship of preacher to people is particularly in danger of becoming a dependent one, as is any helper/helped interaction. The line between helping a person stand on his or her own two feet and seeking to "rescue" that person from life's travail can at times be an exceedingly fine one. The latter is what we want to avoid. Whenever we hear a parishioner say, "Oh, I just don't know what I would do without you," several red flags ought to start flapping vigorously in our faces, despite the warm and pleasant feeling of being needed and useful that such talk arouses. What it should warn us about is the possibility that we have in some ways been doing people's work for them, making them dependent upon us to face what they have to face or think through what they have to wrestle with or tackle those tasks that only they in the end will get either credit or blame for.

Fostering unhealthy dependency happens in a disturbing variety of ways, but I want to describe two well-defined preaching styles that are particularly good at it. I am saying not that there is *nothing* good in these approaches but rather that as a consistent approach and style, repeated time after time, they take their toll on the very interdependence we hope to achieve. As it happens, they represent what some would call two ends of a theological spectrum: positive thinking and social activism.

People want and need good news and affirmation of their strengths. God knows we never suffer from a lack of critics and doomsayers. But that strain of preaching that takes as its unwavering theme the idea that looking on the bright side, thinking positively, holding fast to what feels good *and letting the rest go as unworthy or unreal* is both theologically and psychologically destructive. What happens when, after being buoyed by week after week of positive-thinking preaching, I am smacked in the face with one of life's undeniable negatives—a death, the loss of a job, someone making me furiously and deservedly angry, cruelty? Well, what happens is all too predictable: I must return to the source of this assurance and wisdom, the preacher, for more. I have not been equipped to lead my own life, *inter*dependent with other people, my pastor included; I have been made dependent on the source of a message that, for all its momentary comfort, simply does not square with the real world. It is not terribly surprising that such preachers often have large and loyal followings. The tragedy is that what they might have contributed to a sense of shared community is stolen by the dynamics of false rescue—like persuading a child it can really swim when all you are doing is holding it up and pulling it through the water.

Way over at the other end of the spectrum is preaching that seeks to raise our consciousness about the world's needs and ills—world hunger, war, brutality, all the issues that, of course, any decent person should be concerned about. What happens, though, is that the whole burden of it is placed squarely on our shoulders, sitting there in East Overshoe United Church. Over and over again *we* are made responsible for these things, not in the appropriate sense of needing to know about them and find out what we might possibly do to make a difference but rather in the impossible way of their being made our immediate personal agendas. Yes, I have heard sermon after sermon charge its hearers with both the responsibility for, let us say, world hunger and the mandate to remedy the situation then and there. That, of course, is impossible on both counts. It is one thing to be sensitized to an issue and called to whatever my possible role in it might be; it is something else again to be *given* it and told to set things right single-handedly. The latter, in all its subtle and often compelling variations, is what often happens in preaching, and its net effect is both predictable and destructive: faced with the impossibility of the task, I as a hearer have two choices. Either I can acknowledge that it is baloney and seek a more realistic way into the problem, or I can accept the burden of guilt and begin to lean on the preacher for either absolution or further flagellation, depending on how my mood or personality is leaning at the moment. If I go the latter course, I have become a dependent person, and the preaching made it so or, perhaps worse, tapped into and inflamed what was already a personal predisposition.

Helplessness is closely related to dependency, but the dynamics are a little different, and the way preaching promotes it is not nearly so blatant as in the two examples discussed above. To begin with, we should understand the importance of helplessness as a phenomenon. Studies have shown that when people and animals are made to feel helpless, three things happen: (1) they become depressed, (2) they become progressively less able to learn, and (3) they become physically ill, sometimes to the point of death.[6] You may have had the experience of being "down" (if not outright depressed) and discovering that just *doing* something, whether very successfully or not, made you feel better. That is a mild version of the phenomenon: the less able people are to believe that what they do matters to their fate or their feelings, the more trapped and paralyzed they become. It is a vicious circle: as helplessness increases, so does the ability to learn, which itself might serve to give us back some control and potency.

It does not take a great logical leap to discover that the kind of preaching described a minute ago is sadly long on creating a sense of helplessness. Still more subtly, our best Reformed theology can do the trick when we insist on telling people that because they are accepted by God irrespective of what they do, *nothing they do matters.* Willim Muehl rightly points out that such a message is just about the furthest thing from "good news" we could hear.[7] Telling people that what they do does not count is not and has never been the same thing theologically as saying we are justified by faith; but, judging from what I hear and read, I think it is time for a reminder of the difference.

4. MOVING FROM BLAME TO RESPONSIBILITY

A fourth objective of pastoral preaching is more important than the relatively brief treatment it is getting here might indicate: we can aim to help people take responsibility for their actions. That is a simple enough thing to say, to be sure, but when we realize that it requires a realistic assessment of what we can be responsible for and effective in, the agenda for pastoral preaching grows more complex. Perhaps instead of enjoining people over and over again to do or believe this or that, we might focus on helping them sort out what it is they are, can be, or might become responsible for. I believe a theological case can be made for something like that as the underlying meaning of "repentance": not feeling sorry about our "badness" so much as taking responsibility for our actions.

Engendering guilt is the polar opposite and the potential harm. "Laying a guilt trip" on people, an inelegant though popular phrase, is a wide concern these days and justly so. Not only is guilt destructive in its own right, but it also keeps us from grappling with real responsibility—which, for my money, is a better distinction than trying to make our way through a linguistic briarpatch sorting out "real" or "appropriate" guilt from unnecessary or pathological forms of the same thing.

In preaching, though, we sometimes make people feel guilty about their feelings, forgetting the basic psychological rule that feelings are morally neutral—it is *actions* that we can make ethical judgments about. Sometimes we seek to gain acceptance, affection, and importance by making others feel they are not measuring up to what we really deserve. Sometimes we create guilt by confusing one person's problem with another's: if there is apathy in the congregation about worship, for instance, chances are that berating those people who *are* present and hearing the sermon is pointless.

What I have to remember if I am to grow in responsibility is that I am never "guilty" for doing or not doing something I *could not* have done or avoided doing in the first place. It is not a bad guideline for preachers to use when they begin to talk about responsibility. We want to talk about the "big" issues—life and death, major forces in society, the great themes of biblical faith, justice, war and peace, dehumanization, and all the rest. We want our people to be responsive to those things, to think about them, be moved by them, *do* something about them. All that is as it should be. What we may forget in our exuberance, however, is that though I can be aware of and concerned about the global issues, the limits of my power and *responsibility* are much more tightly drawn.

Pastoral preaching, therefore, wrestles with the conflict between global and life-determining issues, on the one hand, and the finite limits of individual (or congregational) influence, on the other. If we lower our sights too much, we stand justly accused of dodging the gospel's imperatives; but if we aim too high and lay an impossible burden on our people, we risk engendering unnecessary and destructive guilt, *especially if they should happen to believe us*. Somewhere in the interplay between those two poles will be found the domain of real responsibility, and there is probably no better way to lead our people to it through preaching than to confess and seek to enlist their participation in this very struggle.

So far we have talked about four major issues of the help and the harm of preaching. They have all had to do with what we could call "total personal integration," the overall ways people come to see themselves, respond to life's questions and exigencies, and relate themselves to significant other people both individually and in community. Before we turn to five more specific harm/help issues, it is time for a reminder of the underlying message of these paragraphs: the communication tool we use in preaching is enormously powerful, applied week after week to the value structures, hopes, self-identifications, and working commitments of our hearers. I stress this point because I am convinced that some of the harm we do comes from a feeling of impotence, the discouraging sense that what we do in the pulpit is just a drop in the bucket and therefore we had better make each sermon splash as much as it can. It is not unlike the frustration of the counselor, who sees and knows far more about the counselee's life and problem than could possibly be heard and assimilated quickly. Week after week in the counseling room we seem to cover the same ground, trip over the same resistances, agonize over the same intractable problems and patterns of behavior. The temptation grows to cut through it all with one or two mighty swathes of interpretation and direction. Again and again we have to pull ourselves back from doing that with the reminder that the impatience we feel with the slowness of the process and the powerlessness we persuade ourselves is our lot in life are *our* problem, not our people's. Honesty on our parts, the voice of deep conviction, a sense of urgency, a burning desire for people to know and respond—these are all required, all a part of the energy without which preaching hangs limp and lifeless. But they must be informed by our knowing what these sermons do to and for people. Those commitments of ours are of value only when they are working for other people rather than expressing, no matter how righteously, the self-indulgence of our own frustrations.

Let us turn now to five more specific ways preaching either helps or harms: the issues of grief, isolation, expression of feeling, "mystification," and self-esteem. When we finish, we will have a list of nine potent variables (ten would have brought me closer to a homiletical decalogue than I could be comfortable with) that will make up the working context of the chapters to come.

5. MAKING "GOOD GRIEF"

Loss is universal, whether through death of loved human beings, changes in life circumstance, or the slow progress through life's stages, which, no matter what it gains in age and wisdom, is also inevitably a leaving behind of what once was. Response to loss is, of course, one of the central themes of Christian faith, with our emphasis on the resurrection of Jesus Christ and the triumph over death—all kinds of death. Facilitating what Granger Westberg called "good grief"[8] and healthy mourning is an obvious and dominant pastoral objective. Strangely, however, we sometimes do not think of it explicitly as a *preaching* goal. How many of us have actually preached with any regularity on the subject itself? How often has the content of a given sermon been checked and informed by our asking ourselves what it will sound like to someone who is actively grieving?

When studies of death and dying became popular some years ago, stimulated initially by such popular and important writing as that of Elisabeth Kubler-Ross, we grew more aware of how often the grieving process needs active guidance to do its necessary emotional "work." Coping with loss is one of the things we seem to do least well in our contemporary culture. (It is still a safe bet that far too many congregations would not recognize that grieving is also something that inevitably does and should accompany the experience of losses other than and in addition to deaths of loved ones.) The degree to which we have protected people, especially children, from the effects of loss is both encouraging (when we actually have managed to reduce such experiences, for instance, through better health care or more stable community lives) and also alarming (when "protection" has been simply a denial of the facts of life). I recently spoke with a middle-aged minister who was getting ready to relocate from the parish he had served for many years—his first and only one. It was, he said, the first real grief experience he had had. No one in his family had yet died, and he could not recall any major experience of loss. It was a bittersweet realization for him, because while he was glad to have been so lucky, he also knew that he lacked an essential emotional experience and, you could say, skill: learning how to grieve.

Preaching can facilitate good grief by affirming both our belief that death is not the final chapter, even though it is certainly a real one, and our commitment as a Christian community to loan each other the strength and support we sometimes cannot muster from our own reserves. But if we are careless or uninformed, preaching can also interrupt the grieving process and deny our people the natural healing experience of mourning that is surely as much a gift of God as the life that is promised before and after death.

A short catalogue of the ways preaching harms in this respect will be, to many, all too familiar. Sometimes we effectively deny real death, directly or indirectly, by our theologically inaccurate assumption that God sets aside loss. Far too many Christian believers hold a doctrine of immortality rather than of resurrection, and they learned much of it from the preaching they heard. Sometimes we intimate, if we do not come right out and say, that it is somehow unchristian to be sad at loss. People who would be appalled at hearing "Big boys and girls don't cry" are at the same time fully capable of believing that Christians shouldn't. Sometimes we act and talk as though the body were not real to begin with, perhaps in the name of the "spirit," as, for instance, when we arrange funeral practices to eliminate so far as possible any confrontation with the body itself (no "viewings," insistence on "memorial services," forbidding children to attend funerals, and the like). Funerals themselves, together with the sermons that are sometimes preached at them, *can* be helpful pastoral tools for managing grief, but they can also be plain denials. I have heard funerals called "celebrations" or "witnesses of thanksgiving" or "services of joy," virtually forbidding the acknowledgment or expression of what any but the most repressed or unaffected plainly feels: sadness, anger, betrayal, confusion, hopelessness—all the many hues of grief.

We will be returning to this major issue cluster later. For now the point to note is that if Christian preaching has the power to help people grieve more completely and effectively, it also has a history of contributing its fair share to our nearly epidemic inability to cope with loss.

6. FREEING PEOPLE FOR BONDING

We spoke of *koinonia* a bit earlier, but there is a somewhat different aspect of the whole business of life in community that needs a separate point of its own: the question of freeing people from the negative magnetic fields that keep them isolated.

Preaching can play its role in the developmental process called in family therapy circles the growth of "related individuation." All of us strive for a balance between individual autonomy or "self-ness" and a merging of ourselves in close relationships. The great servant imagery of the Bible speaks directly to the matter, particularly Jesus' paradoxical treatments of the roles of servant and master, greater and lesser, in which one finds freedom and identity precisely in giving oneself to another. Where the balance is skewed in one direction or the other, we find the familiar personality types who either are unable to form attachments and relationships to other people or seem to have no identity of their own apart from others with whom they interact—and upon whom they ultimately depend.

So far there are no surprises here, though the achievement of related individuation is sometimes fraught with peril and few of us reach the ideal balance we would like, at least in all circumstances. What has to be said, though, is that inept preaching can all too easily contribute its share to derailing the process, perhaps because the whole subject of how we relate to other people is such a frequent and highly charged topic of preaching (as, indeed, it should be). Sadly, the other side of the coin is that preaching can create isolation from the very relationships it intends to cultivate. This can happen in at least three ways: through privatism, inappropriate self-denial, and suspiciousness of outsiders.

Writers in the area of religion in society have worried for years about the increasing trend in our culture toward privatism and individualism, the pulling apart of those bonds of trust and mutual accountability that form the basis of related individuation and hence, ultimately, of community. Preaching enters the picture with its tendency to use private language and conceptualization, its emphasis on personal fulfillment and salvation, its distrust (particularly, I am afraid, in more conservative circles, though it certainly does not have to be so) of the corporate and the social. Even the most sensitive *pastoral* preaching can veer so far in the direction of individual need and satisfaction as to send the covert message that only the "individuation" part of the equation merits our full attention.

Self-denial is one of those theological staples that sounds unassailable at first. Isn't that what Jesus taught? No, not in the sense I mean. The Bible consistently talks about using one's self for others, about pouring one's own energy and lifeblood into the concerns and perhaps the very existences of other people. It does *not* talk about a blanking out of the self, a "denial" of it. As I write I am thinking of a young woman who had been raised on a steady diet of self-denial: wanting things for oneself, taking care of one's own needs, developing independence of spirit and action were all lumped into the refuse bag of "selfishness." The net result was that while the poor woman had strong and moving desires to help other people, she had no resources of self to bring to the task and was, effectively, paralyzed. She had been taught to cancel her self out rather than to cultivate it for use in the service and lives of fellow human beings. There is a vast difference.

While xenophobia is something we associate more with Russians and Pygmies than fellow church members, a fair amount of it can be found at any Sunday worship service. It can be blatant or subtle, vicious or fawning, brazen or frightened. Anytime our preaching fans people's suspicions of difference, we need to see a flashing red light. Sometimes it is wariness of people who don't use the same theological code we do, sometimes it is such a heavy emphasis on in-house concerns and understandings that "outsiders" are effectively stigmatized, and sometimes it is simply such an unwavering focus on individuals isolated from relationship that the automatically corresponding message is "Beware!"

7. FREEING PEOPLE TO FEEL

Preaching can facilitate the free expression of feeling and the working through of feelings, both positive and negative, so that our people's emotional lives grow richer, more varied, and more accessible. The goal is *not,* I hasten to add, an undisciplined "emoting," 1960s-style perhaps, in which the ultimate objective is to give free reign to every feeling you have at the moment you have it and damn the consequences. No, what I am talking about here is an emotional "facility" through which a person can be directly aware of his or her feelings, take responsibility for them, and choose what is the healthiest and most appropriate action to take as a result of them. For instance, I am not worried if a person *knows* he or she is angry but, given the circumstances, chooses to deal with that anger privately and individually; I am concerned when the person is not able to allow himself or herself to have or to know about the anger in the first place.

We do harm in several ways, again without intending it. To be sure, we sometimes do hear from the pulpit messages whose eventual translation really has to be "You shouldn't feel that way." Every funeral sermon that even indirectly admonishes its hearers not to be sad is guilty of that. More insidious, however, is the tendency preachers have to connect feelings to moral judgments, even in casual speech about whether it is "right" to feel this way or that or about one or another "good" or "bad" feeling. As one who lives in both theological and psycho-therapeutic worlds, I find an especially painful irony and dilemma here. One of the very most basic therapeutic axioms is that feelings are morally neutral, neither right nor wrong, neither good nor bad. Only actions (including, of course, the action of giving overt social expression to a feeling) come into the realm of moral or ethical judgments. My feelings may be appropriate or inappropriate to the situation, negative or posi-tive in their effect on me, useful or counterproductive, and so on through a list of other fine distinctions—none of them moral. Hardly anything is more basic.

On the theological side, however, we are so accustomed to dealing with the states of our attitudes, hearts, inner beliefs, and dispositions that quite often we move squarely to the opposite extreme and wind up saying that feelings are just the very things that count the most in a moral system. I am not really trying to convince anyone here, because we will be returning to this subject later. It can get sticky, especially when dealing with certain seemingly troublesome passages of scrip-ture that talk about the states of people's hearts. For now, my caution is simply that we realize how much damage we can do by blurring the lines between inner feeling and outer action for people who may already be confused about the difference.

8. MAKING LIFE INTELLIGIBLE

In a little book probably not as widely read as it deserves to be, *Preaching in a New Key,* Clement C. Welsh makes a telling point of the difference between preaching as providing infor-mation and preaching as helping people make sense of their lives.[9] The latter is a vital but neglected objective of pastoral preaching: enabling people to interpret their lives meaningfully and intelligibly, even if on the basis of "information" they already have. Notice that that does *not* mean taking the myste-riousness of life in Christian perspective away. Quite to the contrary, what we mean here is helping people live more fully *into* the mystery of God, in its complexity, its suspendedness when questions may have to wait a long time to be married to answers, its refusal to conform its long-range commitments for the human enterprise to our short-range wants and urgings.

The harmful side of the coin is what we could call (in what will at first seem a paradoxical way) "mystification." This too is a term taken from the lexicon of family systems thinking, modified here for our own purposes. By it I simply mean the process whereby life gets turned ever so slightly on its head and seems to be what the "real world" part of us suspects it isn't. Mystery becomes bafflement—not the same thing at all. Mystification seldom stems from anyone's deliberate attempt to mislead. It happens instead when without our being aware of it we alter our perception of reality and, in effect, try to enlist other people's support for it. When, for instance, as a preacher I am angry about something in my own life but take that anger out on my hapless listeners in some way completely irrelevant to my own problem, I am "mystifying" them.

A beautiful example of the process was given me by a navy chaplain. He was about to embark on extended sea duty, and as he was bidding farewell to his family he said to his four-year-old son in a fairly typical and offhanded way, "Now, you take care of Mommy." Instantly the child burst into tears. The chaplain was befuddled. "Why are you crying, dear?" he asked. "Because," the child sputtered, "I *can't* take care of Mommy. I don't know how!" The child was being given an impossible task on the assumption (even if not literal, in this case) that he could do it, and the net result was his "mystification."

So-called double-bind messages are classic ways of mystifying people. In the double bind we give people contradictory instructions, telling them to do one thing overtly but then in other ways (perhaps non-verbally or through half-stated assumptions) forbidding them to do it. I recall a mother who took her teenage son shopping for a sports jacket, insisting that he choose the one *he* wanted because it was time he learned to make his own decisions about such things. When the young man finally made his selection and showed it to his mother, her response was something like "Oh, Curt, I really don't think that's the one you want, do you?" Neat. A game of "reality, reality, who's got the reality?" When in our preaching we enjoin people to do good and take full responsibility for their actions but at the same time tell them on theological grounds that because of human sinfulness they are not capable of doing that, we have "double-bound" and mystified them.

A final means of mystification may sound paradoxical at first: trying to explain life so completely that it holds no paradoxes, mysteries, or conundrums—in effect, trying to demystify it. That too is harmful, along the lines of telling someone that what their eyes plainly see is a puzzle is not really so at all. One classic theological subject with which we try to work that unrealistic sleight-of-hand is theodicy, the pastoral issue of why "bad things happen to good people." I have heard countless sermons on that broad subject, and the only ones that came even close to being good and helpful were those that accepted the essential mysteriousness of theodicy. There are lots of things we can say to help people caught in the throes of it, but when we try to make life patent and smooth and perfectly consistent in the face of its obvious dilemmas, rough-nesses, and inconsistencies, we are asking people to applaud the emperor's new clothes. We are mystifying them by trying to demystify essential mystery. In the process we are cutting against the grain of our hope of helping them live freely within the life-giving mystery of God.

9. HELPING PEOPLE ACCEPT ACCEPTANCE

Simply loving and accepting people is often not enough. Too many people need to be helped to be able to accept their acceptance, so pervasive is the idea in them either that they are just not eligible for it or that such love cannot possibly come without strings attached. Becoming a new and loved person in Jesus Christ is seldom as easy as we preachers often make it sound. What we are aiming for with pastoral preaching is an increase in self-esteem, which I take to mean not only what we feel about ourselves right now but also our capacity increasingly to receive and believe love in the future.

I don't imagine any responsible preacher sets out to lower people's self-esteem, but, unfortunately, it happens anyway and with fair regularity. That is the harmful side of the coin. Continually badgering people about how bad and sinful they are is the most obvious way, but there are more subtle ones. Most of us, for instance, manage successfully to avoid "works righteousness"—putting a price tag on acceptance by demanding certain behavior or activity. What we less easily avoid is a sort of "feelings righteousness," in which the subtle message is that unless our attitudes or emotions are arranged a certain way we cannot expect to be loved and accepted, either by our fellow human beings or by God. Time and again I have heard the message that God will forgive me and meet me "where I am," followed either overtly or implicitly by the additional clause: *provided* I confess in a certain way, participate in the church on a certain pattern, set aside my anger or impatience, or (as we discussed earlier) deny myself as a self. Theologically that does not hold water, and we ought to know it. God's acceptance is unconditional. What I *do* with that, whether I can let it restore my life and change me, may be another matter, depending indeed on how I arrange my responses. But to tell me that "up front" God's love is unconditional *but* requires me to make certain adjustments is to put a price tag on acceptance.

This has been a long and no doubt partly confusing list of assets and liabilities in pastoral preaching. We will be coming back to many of these things in later chapters, where, I hope, they will grow clearer and more manageable. My purpose here has been largely to show you how high the stakes are, what opportunities—both to help and to harm—face us each time we preach. If in the face of it we start thinking twice about what we say, knowing something more of the power we hold as preachers, but in the end continue to speak with both force and humility, then the purpose will have been met.

3. The Restoring Role of Proclamation in Pastoral Preaching I: Is the Preacher Priest or Prophet?

Whenever I talk to ministers or seminary students about pastoral preaching I can be morally certain that one question will come up in discussion. In its most straightforward version it goes something like this: "All well and good, but what about *proclaiming the gospel?* All this talk about personal process notwithstanding, we do have a prophetic Word to preach, don't we?" I do not make light of that at all, even though I have to confess that after a while the question takes on, let us say, a certain "familiarity." Nevertheless, here we have one of the central issues and tensions in preaching, and it needs full treatment. Notice I do not say "answer." It is not so much a matter of answering the question or deciding the issue as one of working responsibly in the midst of a dialectical tension between equally valid and compelling claims on the preacher. To do that well, of course, we must first understand what the issue *is,* and that is a theological task far from as easy as radical partisans of either pole sometimes realize.

Dealing with the tension takes us straight into the middle of the question "What *is* the gospel, that we should be able to talk about it as we do?" Since that is a rather large apple to bite into, we need to divide it (as good preachers do) into more manageable parts. First, we must look at the nature of religious and theological language, both in and out of the Bible—and if working preachers once thought that was a chore best left to the academic theologians, they must think again: it is as pragmatic and present a vocation as running the mimeograph machine.

Second, we need to examine rather closely those venerable images of "priestly" and "prophetic" preaching, to find out what we have really intended to *do* with each of them. I will tell you now that I believe we preachers have been laboring under a false dichotomy and that it is time for a more unified and consistent point of view. Third, we want to reexamine the functions of pastoral preaching, setting aside the stereotypes and interrogating the common assumptions with which we have worked. In the next chapter I am going to try to make the point that many supposed conflicts between "pastoral" and "proclamatory" preaching have all too often been false—the result of a carelessness with both language and communicative purpose rather than of any real theological difference.

GOD-TALK: THE SILENT LANGUAGE

"The Silent Language" was the title of a pioneer study in nonverbal communication, written by Edward T. Hall.[1] The book itself is a classic and well worth reading; however, it is only the image of its title that I want to borrow here, because it introduced us to a then-revolutionary idea: there are "languages" other than the everyday verbal descriptions we are most commonly aware of, and they are at least as powerful in their communicative influence as our more familiar stock-in-trade speech. The central thesis of this discussion is this: *the role and function of theological language is more interpretative than it is descriptive*. That perhaps innocent-seeming distinction carries a great deal of weight for our understanding of preaching, especially from the perspective of pastoral communication.

The differences between "description" and "interpretation" are largely what you would expect from ordinary usage of the terms. When we use language descriptively, we are using it to *refer to* something, in order to reproduce for a hearer or reader a more or less accurate picture of what we are talking about. We have in our heads an experience we want a receiver of our communication also to have, and so we describe it as best we can to that purpose—whether what we are describing is an object, an event, a state of mind, a characteristic, or what have you. It is the *referential* capacity of language that allows us to do that descriptive work, and it is probably our commonest use of words.

Interpretation is rather different, though the two categories are by no means watertight compartments. When we use language interpretatively, our intention is not to describe something so much as to make sense of it, to unpack its meaning, to "place" both ourselves and our hearers in the scene of it. Most likely we will use categories of thought that do not themselves point to anything in a referential sense so much as they articulate connections and relationships among things, and of course those categories are expressed in language— interpretative rather than descriptive language. In psycho- therapy, for example, a great deal of time is spent by both client and therapist in the descriptive mode, talking about the events of a person's history, current experience, relationships, inner thoughts and dreams, and the like. From time to time, however, the mode shifts as the therapist endeavors to formulate what some particular combination of things may *mean* to the experi- ence of the client. That is interpretation.

Here, however, enters a complication: the act of interpreta- tion itself becomes an event of sorts, at least a linguistic happening, that can now be referred to in a descriptive way, as when I might say, "Do you recall my saying last week that going down staircases seems to remind you of the painfulness of leaving home?" That, of course, is how the communication process itself works: a message (which is an encoded event) becomes an event in its own right that gets referred to in yet another message, and so on down the line like Chinese boxes. The process works quite efficiently, *provided* some part of our thinking continues to monitor (not necessarily in a self-con- scious or explicit way) which generation of experience we are talking about. Trouble can arise when the monitoring process slips a cog and we begin to refer to a message about something as though it were that primary event itself, as, for instance, with rumors.

Trouble of the same order, but far more difficult to correct, sets in when we confuse description and interpretation. On communicative grounds we could say that the confusion is between empirical eventfulness and meaningfulness, or between object and significance. Theologically, things are a bit more serious, for when we lose the descriptive/interpretative distinction we begin to speak of God as *object* and of transcendence as everyday observable experience. One illustration of that is the troublesome, though common, syntactical expression "of God." Heaven knows how often we use the phrase: will of God, love of God, justice of God, presence of God, hand of God, people of God—the list is endless. I'm not trying to ban its use, of course, only to look at a pitfall it opens up. When we are careful, we use that phrase interpretatively: something in our experience takes on a significance far beyond the humdrum everyday, and we want to "refer" it to God, as Diogenes Allen says.[2] But when we are not careful, the language slips ever so quietly into the descriptive mode and we talk as though this something-of-God were a part of our world of object relations that could be seen, referred to, and grasped *directly* as we would any other human experience. When that happens, our mode of discourse has gone fundamentally off the theological track and the radical, transcendent otherness of God has been lost.

When I argue that theological language is more interpretative than descriptive, it is precisely this distinction—and this danger—that I have in mind. We use theological language not to describe transcendent reality directly but rather to interpret a dimension of our experience we claim extends beyond the mundane world of sight and sound. What such language "describes," to be technically correct, is a dimension of significance rather than an array of "objects," and that adds up to a working definition, at least, of interpretation. We can think of it as a "silent language."

So far as the "debate" between proclamation and pastoral preaching is concerned, the point I am making here is simple: if by "proclamation" we have meant (perhaps without realizing it) an attempt to *describe* the transcendent reality of God and his work without taking into account the crucial difference between interpretation and description, then we have been off base on both communicative and theological grounds. It is no contest; that is not what pastoral communication does, *but it is not what "proclamation" is or does either*. Put another way, I do not believe we have direct descriptive access to God; we *do* have a direct connection with the meaningfulness, the impact, the significance of that mysterious dimension of our (and that of our predecessors in faith) experience which we believe is the inbreaking of God's being and work.

What then, does theological language do, as the preacher uses it? Several crucial things, I would say, and I would further argue that these are "proclamation" in the fullest sense, fully consistent with the pastoral agenda. Let me list five key aspects, none of which have to do with "describing transcendent reality."

First, theological language binds us into a community of faith and meaning. It establishes a connectedness, through common usage and understanding, with other periods and other people, as well as knitting us more closely with our contemporaries in both our affirmations of faith and our life journeys. People who *talk* the same in some very important senses *are* the same; they are members of a community. The more intimate and momentous the talk, the more closely integrated is the community.

Second, as Ian Ramsey has argued, theological language articulates the "oddity," the "what is seen and more" quality of our religious or transcendent experience.[3] Paradoxically, if we try to make theological language ordinarily descriptive, we lose its working dynamic, which is to lift up the almost inexpressible, mysterious, life-determining dimension of experience in which we want to say, "God is at work." Whenever

I use the phrase "of God," to return to our earlier example, I have a sense that I am in the presence of something far beyond my power to imagine or apprehend, at the same time as I sense that life is being shaped and offered in ways beyond my or any human being's power to accomplish.

Third, not only does theological language articulate the transcendent dimension of experience, but it also provides what I would call an interpretative framework for it. We will return to the concept of framing later in this chapter. For now, suffice it to say that what we perceive in a picture is partly determined by how it is framed (which is why I pay three times as much money to have my rather meager works of art framed by a sensitive professional rather than take them to the local frame-it-yourself center). I sense that my life is lived out in a narrative framework that gives it location and dimension and emphasis and that mediates a future I do not have to fear as being fundamentally against me; theological language is the way I have of establishing that framework. It is not that the picture itself is so very different from anyone else's—the same minor victories, lost loves, vexing dilemmas, niblets of hope, and all the rest—so much as that the framework which lets me interpret and place that picture is unique.

Fourth, theological language offers a *perspective on* reality because it gives an information-processing schema or filter through which comes the unending stream of sense experience that makes consciousness. When I "look at life theologically," as we sometimes put it, that does not mean I have a separate and sacralized version of reality but rather that the very categories and processes of my thinking are influenced by faith commit-ment. The language gives me those categories; it does not generate a different body of experiential data.

Finally, theological language possesses a gravitational qual-ity; it invites me to "come and see." It pulls me out of my common frame of reference and teases me into a curiosity about what lies beyond it, about the strange Galilean of whom it was also said, when all attempt at explanation failed, "come and see." In short, it reminds me that if I stop searching and growing I am functionally dead, and that was not, so far as we can tell, God's aim.

Now, briefly, let me just translate those five functions of "proclamation" into another language system. When as a human being I am able to function in a community of shared value and meaning; when I am able to talk about and expose myself to ambiguity, uncertainty, and mystery; when I am able to perceive the surrounding framework of value and significance of my life, so as to trust the future to be working with rather than against the grain of life; when I am appropriately self-conscious about the very thought and feeling categories I use to arrange the "data" of my life; and when I am able to let myself respond to the "pull" of hope and opportunity—when I am able to do all those things, I have the potential for living what we would call, on psychological grounds, a whole and healthy life. I offer that as an initial bid for saying that proclamation and pastoral preaching interact on the basis of a shared foundation, available to build on if we understand the nature of theological language from an interpretative angle. Let us, then, try to set aside the facile and inaccurate stereotype that "proclamation" talks about God while "pastoral" communication deals only with the human. Neither is what the gospel, as good news about the ultimate reality of life, ever was.

IS THE PREACHER PRIEST OR PROPHET?

We will be returning to this distinction between so-called priestly and prophetic roles in preaching when we come to the discussion of conflict and confusion in chapter 8. For now, however, we need to look at it from the vantage point of our opening question: Where in pastoral perspective is there room for the prophetic word of proclamation?

Let us first get a rather unpleasant business out of the way. Our yearning for what we call "prophetic" preaching is sometimes a thinly disguised appeal for inappropriately getting some of our own needs met in the pulpit. It happens to the best of us from time to time, though for some of us it has become an unfortunate style that really needs direct intervention and help. I am recalling lots of conversations, my own and others', and here is what they say.

Sometimes we are just plain angry (at all kinds of things, sometimes relevant to our congregations, sometimes not), and since some part of us says that for the preacher to get angry in the pulpit is forbidden, we adopt a substitute strategy. We preach "prophetically," sometimes with great vigor, about how our people have botched the job with their stiff-necked, callous, and idolatrous ways. We may *say* "we" a lot in such sermons, and we may even link them to the most righteous of personal or social causes. But to a less inducted observer, the unmistakable message of misplaced anger comes through.

Ironically, there *is* a place for anger in the pulpit, if we would only learn to use it. There are many things in this world about which I as a preacher *should* be angry, as should my people. Preaching that expresses, interprets, and harnesses the motive power of that anger is both vital and difficult. It is essential to the ministry of healing. It is also very different from beating one's congregation verbally about the head and shoulders because they are not moving fast enough in your direction, or because your kids are driving you crazy, or because some shallow-minded pulpit colleague down the road has reduced the gospel to a shopping list of psychological helps and hints and you are afraid of guilt by association.

Sometimes, too, we are frustrated about the often painfully slow process of ministry and think that a little more "straight talk" will speed things up. "Isn't there a time," we ask, "when people need to set aside their developmental agendas and their complicated feelings or relationships and hear what God wants them to get on with in their lives?" Of course. But the chances are good, I have found, that when such a message arises out of a sense of mounting frustration and anger in the preacher, that may be precisely the *wrong* time for it. There is a vast difference, in other words, between prophecy (in either a biblical or a general theological sense) and pique or petulance. Maybe the thing to watch for is whether my frustration is truly *on behalf of my people,* with their growth and faith as the dominant concern, or on behalf of myself (with perhaps a dash or two of self-pity thrown in for flavor).

A gnawing sense of impotence can also drive us into a false distinction between pastoral and prophetic stances. Sometimes we feel we are just not getting through, and although that may lead us to frustration with others, it may instead leave us with the feeling of our own weakness, rather a different reaction. Much of our talk about ministerial leadership in recent years has focused on *change*—how to bring it about, why it is needed, and so forth—and we may have gotten an unrealistic and slightly romantic notion of how rapidly or pervasively change comes about. It is not hard for preachers to give themselves pretty low marks because they seem to be woefully ineffective "change agents," especially from the pulpit; that despair can bring about a flight into what I would have to call the "pseudo-prophetic."

The same thing happens among psychotherapists, interestingly enough, and for a good sense of perspective a preacher feeling his or her impotence at the task might want to read Janet Malcolm's book *Psychoanalysis: The Impossible Profession.*[4] It is the report of an extensive series of interviews with a prominent (though anonymous) psychoanalyst, in which the analyst confesses his realization that people change far less and far less easily than he once believed. In the end, though, owning up to that is not a counsel of despair so much as a call for us to look again at our basic change orientation and some of its theological presumptions. Two such presumptions that seem common among preachers are (1) that the timing of things is earthbound and, while a thousand years in God's sight may be as a watch in the night, it's a hell of a long wait for those of us on twenty-four-hour days, and (2) that effecting change is somehow the work of the preacher rather than that of the community itself or that of God in and through even our most impotent efforts.

Then, too, there is the ever-present phenomenon of professional burnout (subtly different, again, from either frustration or impotence, though obviously related), which can lead us either into selling life insurance or into disastrously intensified pulpit efforts to set the prophetic record straight once and for all—as a friend of mine says he once wrote, tongue-in-cheek, in the margin of a sermon manuscript, "Point obscure; pound the pulpit and shout like hell!" Burnout itself is to be taken seriously, especially for helping professionals. In preaching it can lead to an increasing stridency of tone and demandingness of content, sometimes masked by our claim that we are being "prophetic" or "proclamatory" when in fact we are trying desperately to compensate for growing feelings of ennui and helplessness.

Having gotten that rather tedious business out of the way, I need now to say that the more legitimate and honestly felt urgency to proclaim the gospel "in season and out of season" is to be taken seriously. The question is, do we really have to choose between the roles of prophet and priest?

For the sake of perspective we need to review briefly what usually seems to be meant in the distinction between prophetic (proclamatory) and priestly (pastoral) preaching, having set aside in the previous paragraphs some of the commonest distortions. Despite a whole range of factors involved, three primary variables seem to account for most of the differences: (1) the kind of language used, (2) the direction of attention of the message, and (3) the nature of the addressee. Depending on how we handle those three things, we will come up with one kind of preaching or the other, on traditional terms.

1. The *kind of language* used takes us back to the beginning distinction between interpretation and description. "Prophetic" models of preaching will be found stressing the biblical-theological language of God's mighty acts and the responses sought from humankind: worship, repentance, faithfulness, servanthood, etc. "Priestly" preaching, by contrast, stays more within

the human experiential domain, with an emphasis on human need and healing.

2. The *direction of attention of the message* is a factor expressed by the popular psychological distinction of "outer" vs. "inner-directed." The proclamatory direction of attention is outward, to mission, to a world in need of confrontation and change, or to individual behavior that violates the gospel's standards of acceptability. The pastoral model, by contrast, has tended to direct its attention inward, to the condition of the human beings addressed.

3. The *nature of the addressee* takes us into a distinction between a corporate and an individual focus of attention. The prophetic stance addresses the church as a corporate entity, the body of Christ, and it frequently rails against the privatization and individualization that seem to characterize our culture. The pastoral address is typically more individual, even when it is concerned with relationships and group life.

Now, if you run your finger down those two lists you come up with what I suggest are the prevailing "models" for the two approaches in preaching. "Prophetic" means preaching about God's being and activity, directing our attention to the mission of Christian faith and action in a desperate world, and calling on the church as organic entity to find itself and respond. "Priestly" means preaching about human brokenness and travail, directing us to the need for inner renewal and strength, addressing us as individual children of God being sought by a Lord who loves us as he does every sparrow that falls. In other words, if you take any biblical-theological concern—love, justice, freedom, discipleship, servanthood, hope, repentance, and so on—and apply each pole of those three variables to it, you will come up with a different communicative approach, falling more or less clearly into one dominant paradigm or the other. Obviously, this is an embarrassingly condensed account of a lot of historical and homiletical material, not without the risk of setting up a straw person. Nevertheless, in both practice and argument this is what appears to me to be the dominant lineup of issues and choices underlying the fear that preaching as pastoral communication misses its proclamatory mandate. The question is what we do with that.

All too often, I fear, we have acted as though what we had to do was *choose* one approach over the other. Having done so, we have then sometimes fallen into the trap of assuming that when talking in one predominant mode we were automatically rejecting the other: that is the backlash of adopting a logic of *choice* to begin with. One more step is sometimes taken: a minister finding himself or herself tending to stay with one side of the lineup or the other comes to believe that to switch over to the other would be a theological betrayal or inconsistency, and so the paradigms harden and the division grows more rigid.

This book, of course, is adopting a different course altogether, which you have already begun to see. My argument is that there is nothing wrong with the three variables themselves and that seeing the different approaches to them as hard choices to be made—on theological grounds, at that—is what causes the trouble. Instead of choices, I would suggest that they are dialectical tensions built into the nature of things and that to close down the tension is to lose the very thing we are trying to be faithful to. In the nature of dialectic, as soon as we veer too far toward one polarity, the other calls us back again. It is not a "conflict" to be "resolved" but a dynamic interaction to be sustained.

We need, in other words, to move away from the kind of talk that pulls us into artificial conflict and to find a way of expressing the convictional unity that grows out of the dialectical differences we so easily observe. Granted, we can easily get lost in a briarpatch of terminology, but perhaps it would be helpful to think of those variables under different names.

Several years ago, I set about trying to get some leverage on the question of what it is in certain communication that raises its impact to the level of "therapeutic" in the clinical domain and "religious" in the theological. Clearly *something* happens when communication reaches the degree of significance or momentousness that distinguishes it from ordinary, mundane stuff and makes it in some way life-determining. The theory I emerged with after examining a lot of messages with an eye out for the inner, systematic features was rather simple. My hunch was (and is) that communication departs from the ordinary and becomes either "therapeutic" or "religious," depending on the perspective we are taking on it, when, at the same time, it is *optimally self-involving, ambiguous, and intense.* When, because of explicitly religious aims and language, we are in the theological world, those factors translate themselves into three other, corresponding qualities of communication: *ethical authority, transformational power,* and *a sense of transcendence.*

That tripartite schema seemed to offer at least the beginning of a *formal* way to describe just what characterized therapeutic and/or religious communication. Naturally, I was curious whether anyone seemed to agree with me or had thought along those same lines. Several parallel systems surfaced, related to but not explicitly about communication itself. Paul Ricoeur had written of the symbolic process that a parable occurs when three factors coincide: (1) a personally meaningful narrative form, (2) the metaphoric process with its built-in tension between representation and embellishment (its "semantic impertinence," as he calls it), and (3) the context of talking not about ordinary things but rather about the "limit experiences" or boundary conditions of human life.[5] With a somewhat similar concern, Stephen Crites wrote a journal article that still stands as a classic, in which he argued that a religious symbol emerges at the intersection of three "tracks" of experience: (1) the "mundane story" of one's own personal existence, (2) the "temporal form" of a tension between past and future, (3) a recognition of the eruption in one's life of the "sacred story" of what is ultimately real and significant.[6] (A semihistorical footnote may be in order. This writing and thinking was being done just as the idea of "narrative" in theology and preaching was beginning its rise to the popularity it holds today as both a concept and an approach to communication. In a sense, what we were all trying to do was find out what intrinsic factors gave narrative its special power.)

Yet a third system that seemed to feed into this growing convergence of thought was Thor Hall's critique of homiletics, in the course of which he discussed what he called "the dynamics of authentic knowing" (or of "real communication," with an indebtedness to Marshall McLuhan).[7] Though in considerably less detail than in the other systems, Hall cited three factors that made for such authenticity: personal participation, involvement, and commitment.

Here, then, from several slightly different language systems and theoretical perspectives we had what still appears to be a remarkably convergent attempt to describe or map the characteristics of communication that the clinician would call therapeutically significant and the theologian would name as religiously important. It needs to be kept in mind that we are not now talking about semantic content but rather about formal characteristics of messages—the way the semantic contents arrange themselves and operate representationally, whether they are explicitly religious, psychological, or what have you.

Table 1: A COMMUNICATION CONVERGENCE

Therapeutic Communication	Parable	Religious Symbol	Authentic Knowledge	Religious Communication
Self-Involvement	Narrative Form	Mundane Story	Participation	Ethical Authority
Ambiguity	Metaphoric Process	Temporal Form	Involvement	Transformational Power
Intensity	Limit Experience	Sacred Story	Commitment	Sense of Transcendent

When I first described the three variables involved in the prophetic/priestly preaching dichotomy, I had put the earlier schema out of conscious thought. Now, though, it clearly looks like the same sort of structure, and perhaps thinking of it in that way offers us a way out of being forced into false choices.

The question of the kind of language used seems to be a question of self-involvement, of how we best join and participate in the mundane real world, which we believe God created and gave into our keeping, a world offered to us in the narrative form of present reality, past history, and future possibility—a question of how we take and discharge *ethical authority* for it. Conscious participation in that world is a byplay between theological interpretation and experiential description, between what we believe about the work of God as wholly other and what we experience as the immediacy of our own often broken existence. Rather than a choice between God-talk and the language of human experience, the issue is sustaining self-involvement in what, from the Christian perspective, we hold to be the "really real" and doing so with a sense of personal significance, as free as we can manage it from defense, denial, or distance.

The direction of address can now be thought of not so much as a question of inner or outer direction, as of sustaining the creative ambiguity of our involvement in the transformational power of God, expressed always in the tension of metaphoric language and image. Surely no one could imagine being fully involved in that transformational world either by retreating wholly within or by spreading oneself so completely onto outer concerns that there was nothing left of self in the process. The very temporal form of the process sustains the dialectic in its tension between past (intrinsically an "outer" matter of history) and future (intrinsically an "inner" category of unrepresented possibility).

Translating the third variable, the nature of the addressee, into this new terminology seems at first improbable, since it apparently involved nothing more difficult than the distinction between individual and corporate focus. Actually, however, something else has probably been going on all along within that distinction, viz., a concern for addressing whatever we take to be the most significant locus of response, or, biblically speaking, for finding "whomever has ears to hear." If that is the point, then the new vocabulary of intensity and mediation of a sense of transcendence through sacred story is even better than the other, sociologically tinged language. In both prophetic and priestly modes, in other words, we have wanted to address the limit conditions of life, securing from our hearers a commitment to examining and perhaps transcending them.

Where, then, have we gotten to? My hope is that as we begin to think along these lines, the dominant concern will be for cultivating those communicative factors that make for the "high moment" of life-determining communication sought by both priest and prophet. I hope we will come to see that on both theological and psychodynamic grounds they are not divided by two different "roles," after all, and still less by different "kinds" of preaching. The effort needs to go elsewhere, to the maintenance of optimal self-involvement, ambiguity, and intensity, and that inevitably requires preserving the tensive interaction between theological and experiential, outer- and inner-directed, corporate and individual. Here is my final summation: *If we should by chance succeed in preaching wholly on one side or the other, we would so distort reality as to foreclose the communicative work of the very things we wish to cultivate.*

I myself will not much miss the prophet/priest distinction. At the risk of seeming simplistic I must still say that there is no evidence that Jesus himself worried about that particular issue. Quite the contrary, what impresses us about what little we know of his work is its underlying congruency and unity. There is a *style* about the man that is far more significant than something trivial like "manner" or "method." In his dealings with people a consistent process appears to be at work that again and again shows itself to have two interlocking phases: (1) nurturing them into an integrated sense of who they truly are and can be as children of God, and (2) leading them to take responsibility both for themselves and for the piece of the world that is given into their care. Over and over again you find people who encounter Jesus being healed and then being sent out to some work or witness; being called to repentance and then being commissioned with a job to do; being taught a new perspective on life and then being energized to put that perspective into operation. There is *movement* to what he does; as Shirley Guthrie reminds us, Jesus does not accept people where they are just for acceptance' sake but rather in order to move them along to someplace else.[8]

Inescapably I am reading my own agenda into what I find in the Bible; but what impresses me is that, at least in Jesus' ministry, *the prophet/priest distinction simply is not there*. What leaps out at us instead is this involvement in a "healing motion" from nurture to responsibility, and on modern terms it can as easily and literally be called therapeutic as proclamatory. That, I believe, is the underlying unity we seek in preaching. If you take nurture alone, you have a form of narcissism; responsibility by itself gives you works righteousness. Together, however, they are something very different, an organic whole that strikes me as being, if anything I have ever heard is, "good news." Need we remind ourselves of Freud's famous dictum about the ultimate goal of emotional health—"to love and to work"?

Here is an image about the role of explicit theological proclamation in preaching. It comes from the world of art, painting in particular, and looks like this: Proclamation of the gospel is not what you mainly see on a canvass. What first grips us is simply the scene, in whatever artistic mode, and if it is good art we are able to recognize in some fashion that it is a scene of our own existence. There is, though, in this art form of "proclamation" something else that leads us strangely beyond the obvious. It is, let us imagine, the brush pattern, or the perspective, or the coloration, or the very style of the content. The gospel is most often that brush pattern; it is seldom the content of the scene. To what will be a picture of ordinary life— even in its extraordinariness—we bring a stroke of the brush, a shifting of the perspective. *That* is the proclamation. *That* is what nurtures us to responsibility, making the difference between art and ornamentation.

4. The Restoring Role of Proclamation in Pastoral Preaching II: What Pastoral Communication Does

I have been arguing in these paragraphs that some of the fear of the absence of proclamation in pastoral preaching arises from a misunderstanding of what theological language is and does. Similar confusion sometimes exists about the functions of pastoral communication: too many of us are working with a caricature rather than an accurate picture of what they are. My hope here again is that some of the uneasiness about the proclamation issue will dissolve once we see more clearly what goes on when we preach from the perspective of pastoral care and concern.

It really is a shame that sometimes people who ought to know better portray pastorally oriented preaching as a thin soup of subjectivism whose ultimate object is just to make people "feel better." What nonsense! (Writing a book is a relatively calm activity, but even now I have to wrestle back the temptation to reply to such a distortion by saying something like "Of course, then, the purpose of biblical preaching is just to entertain people with quaint stories from ancient Near Eastern folklore, with the hope that occasional hints for clean living might be gleaned.")

What is it, then, that pastoral preaching at its best does? Here I want to draw some explicit parallels between preaching and therapeutic situations. I want to look at the functions of pastoral preaching in direct parallel with the functions of psychotherapy—whether "practiced" in the form of pastoral care by ministers or treatment by professional therapists. I am assuredly *not* suggesting, however, that preaching is a "form of therapy," still less that therapy is the place for preaching. Harry Emerson Fosdick's famous dictum that preaching was "pastoral counseling on a good scale"[1] is catchy but misleading, for all its historical value in alerting us to a neglected dimension of the preaching experience.

Perhaps an autobiographical note will clarify my intention. As I regularly practiced both preaching and therapy I fell to wondering whether I really put on two very different professional hats as I moved from one activity to the other. The settings, language, religious orientation of recipients, even my own institutional identifications were very different—something like an exaggeration of the differences of role a minister experiences when he or she shifts from counseling to preaching. Yet I was the same person, and more and more it became clear that the long-range goals I held for both hearers and clients were related—if not the same. What, though, about the work itself? Leaving aside the obvious surface differences between the two activities, were there some deeper commonalities or convergences of *function* between them? In time I came to see that indeed there were—markedly and surprisingly so, in at least four respects: (1) the activity of the preacher or therapist, (2) the nature of the therapeutic and communicative environment, (3) the relationship or alliance between people and practitioner, and (4) the question of therapeutic objectives. Understanding each of those is my argument, then, for what proclamation is and does in pastoral preaching.

WHAT THE PREACHER/THERAPIST DOES

There is little mystery in what a therapist actually does when he or she works. Whether relatively silent or loquacious, direct or oblique, active or passive, in the end the therapist (a) gives permission for some things, (b) reframes issues, and (c) teaches communication. What the therapist clearly does *not* do is take over the work of the client in understanding, feeling, and integrating the impact of the therapeutic experience on real life. That is pretty close to the bottom line, and I see no need to get

unnecessarily fancy with it, though of course the actual practice can be quite complex.

"Giving permission" is sometimes quite explicit, as, for
instance, when I say to a client, "You know it is perfectly all
right to express your anger at me; it won't hurt me and you
might find it helpful to you." More often, perhaps, permission
giving is subtle and implicit, a matter of tone and style and
growing confidence as the therapeutic relationship unfolds. As
a therapist I try to make it possible for the person I am working
with to feel things that have been pushed back before; to let
himself or herself experience more fully and consciously what
is going on in both inner and outer worlds; to look at things
from different angles and in new lights; to confront what he or
she believes is taboo in order for personal values and priorities
to develop free from magical expectations or fears. It sounds
like a simple, perhaps even simple-minded thing. I assure you it
is not. The older and more experienced I get both as a minister
and as a therapist, the more awed I become by what strikes me
as the incredible daily heroism of ordinary people trying to lead
reasonably satisfactory lives against the odds that personal
history and modern society throw against them. The heroism
has a price: it requires the relinquishment of a lot of freedom
and experience just to keep the show together. The therapist
gives permission to reclaim, at least in the relative safety of the
therapeutic experience itself, some of what has had to be set
aside. Permission has to be *given* because the difficult business
of living through any twenty-four-hour period often will not
let people take it for themselves—there is simply not that much
margin for error. I have used a code term for the process; as a
minister I could just as easily have said, with, I believe, complete accuracy, that what we are doing is giving a "blessing."

"Reframing issues" is a concept we encountered earlier when
talking about theological language. It comes from the family
therapy movement, but I find it a more universal metaphor
than that. The basic idea, as we saw, is that the framework of
something—whether a painting hanging on the wall, the fence
around the garden, or the attitude of dread I carry with me to

nearly all holiday cocktail parties—influences the experience of whatever is inside it. Changing the frame somehow affects the content, at least so far as our experience of it is concerned. When we speak of "reframing issues" in psychotherapy we are talking about reinterpreting certain outlooks or assumptions people have used to "frame" or make sense of various things they have encountered. So, for instance, a family with a rebellious and trouble-prone teenager comes for help on the assumption that the "problem" is an out-of-control child, perhaps a "bad" kid. That is the "frame." The therapist may see things quite differently, however, perceiving (for instance) that the child is performing the function of an unconscious light-ning rod, taking on family conflicts and problems and express-ing them with misbehavior so that they are drained away from the family's overall life. When the therapist points out that while the child's behavior is clearly what it is and is not to be condoned, it is stemming from this kind of unconscious family dynamic rather than any intrinsic "badness," then he or she is "reframing the issue." As another example, I once had a client who complained of not having any friends, when in fact, I found as I looked back over what he had told me about himself, there were friends aplenty. I "reframed" the issue by pointing out that he had lots of friends but was uncomfortable being intimate with people, especially the friends he in fact had. The troublesome behavior, while the same as before, began to look quite different when seen in the framework of an internal problem with intimacy rather than an external social situation of "having no friends."

What could we call that in theological terms? The image that comes most dominantly to mind is perhaps a surprising one: "reframing" an issue is what we commonly mean by "proph-esying." Even in classical biblical terms, what the prophet does is not so much forecast the future as take a look at things-as-they-are and point out different connections and meanings from what most people are seeing—precisely what the thera-pist does when he or she reframes an issue or situation. The prophecy may be good news or bad, depending on one's perspective. When an Old Testament prophet points out that what seems an expedient political alliance is in fact inviting disaster, that is unwelcome news. But when Jesus says, "The Kingdom of God is among you," the thrust is very different, pointing to good news that we were not previously able to recognize.

That the therapist teaches communication almost goes without saying, but perhaps we had better at least touch on it. One of the commonest complaints, for instance, of couples coming in for marital counseling is that they have a "communication problem." Usually neither they nor the counselor have the remotest idea what that means, true though it may prove to be. A typical communication difficulty that comes out is the "style" of what I would call mutual diagnosis, in which each spouse is forever commenting on the other's behavior and making a judgment about what it means, where it comes from, or how inappropriate it is rather than expressing what they themselves experience of it. As long as that continues, the fires of conflict will be fanned and we will never get an accurate picture of just what is in fact *going on* with the couple, so taken up are they in premature interpretation and judgment of each other. As therapist I must, in effect, teach them a new communication approach, call it a self-descriptive, nonjudgmental one for lack of better terms. Or again, with virtually any form of therapy a client must be taught how to relax his or her tendency to censor and edit what they say for the therapist's benefit. Saying "whatever comes to mind" is, of course, the hallmark of psychodynamic treatment, and it can be a tough skill to learn, so accustomed are we to cleaning up our acts for public consumption. The list goes on: with highly rational people, I may have to teach the communication of feelings; with intensely pragmatic folks I may need to cultivate the value of "what if" and fantasy-oriented communication; with those with sharply judgmental styles I have to teach how to be plainly descriptive; with people who are frozen in fear of forbidden feelings the teaching needs to be in the direction of freer expression with an emphasis on the crucial difference between feelings and actions.

The theological version of teaching communication is catechesis or, in the biblical sense, *didache*. That is not the whole meaning of *teaching* in theological perspective, of course, but a rather neglected proportion of even classical *didache* strikes me as having at least as much to do with communication skill and style as with theological content. There are communicative qualities of directness, interpersonal empathy, freedom from judgment, personal openness, honest expression of difficulties that plainly seem to characterize the Christian style of "being in the world." They are the kinds of things the church teaches her people, and preaching is a major forum for that kind of learning.

Notice what we have here: squarely *within* the category of pastoral work are the three classical categories of ministry whose supposed conflict this chapter is trying to undermine: priestly or pastoral work in "blessing"; prophetic or proclamatory ministry in "prophecy"; and the educational, didactic function in "*didache*." Please bear in mind that I am not aiming to *reduce* their real differences in order to achieve a false peace. I am rather trying to show that an underlying unity binds them together in ways we have sometimes overlooked in what both preacher and pastor do.

THE NATURE OF THE THERAPEUTIC ENVIRONMENT

Two characteristics of what is usually called the therapeutic environment seem dominant and are directly related to a comparison with pastoral preaching: (1) its "moratorium" quality, and (2) the way it gives responsibility.

We have talked briefly before and will again about the "sanctuary" function of worship and pastoral preaching, and that is also basically what I mean here. The therapeutic space has the quality of a time-out from daily concerns, paradoxically even though those concerns are usually the reason for being there in the first place. The key is that no "acting out" goes on in the therapy. A person is free to deal with all kinds of feelings, past history, desires, impulses, and relationships, secure in the knowledge that this is the occasion for *talking* about them, not *doing* them. In other words, action consequences are temporarily disconnected from what a person says, thinks, and feels. A client can think and talk about his murderous rage toward his wife, because at least in this place the thinking and talking are not going to lead either to action or to any reactions from his spouse.

Another dimension of this sanctuary quality is the reliability of the experience: barring emergencies or periodic adjustments that have to be made, a person knows that in the therapy a particular time, place, and person are his or hers and that the structure of that experience is going to be comfortably the same each time it happens. Beginning therapists sometimes have a hard time learning the importance of that structure to the therapeutic process itself. I myself belong to that school of therapy that places a primary emphasis on the boundaries of the structure; but even approaches that are less picky about it still give it its due. We start and stop on time; we meet in the same location; the client has my undivided attention with no interruptions or distractions; I can be counted on to behave in basically the same way each hour; and the very physical nature of the counseling place, while it may be warmly personal, does not telegraph my own agendas, interests, or extratherapeutic concerns in competition with the client's. Here, in short, is a sanctuary, a place of refuge, and if both client and therapist use it wisely, a person will be strengthened in his or her return to the buffeting forces of the real world outside.

I believe that this same function is served by pastoral preaching and, equally important, the worship context in which it occurs. Think for a minute, for instance, about the sometimes comic resistance congregations are famous for putting up to even minor changes in the order of worship. I vividly recall going to work as a congregation's student assistant and quickly learning that the Worship Committee was reputed to be on the verge of proposing some controversial changes in the order of worship. Great uneasiness was in the air. With some careful sleuthing I was able to get an advance peek at the inflammatory recommendations. They were three in number: the relocation of the offertory to a point after, rather than before, the sermon; the elimination of one midservice hymn; and the introduction of a relatively minor liturgical rubric that I no longer recall (something on the magnitude of adding a "passing of the peace"). For this we were on the eve of revolution?! Yes, and for very good reason: even though this congregation no doubt had its problems elsewhere that were being expressed piggyback on the worship issue, the more obvious thing was that the sanctuary experience was being tampered with, and no matter what the content of those changes might be, the sheer fact of newness was enough to set people on edge. Perhaps less dramatically, I have seen pastors and worship committees plunge into liturgical innovation and variety thinking to bring new excitement to what had become hidebound or jaded, only to discover that some quality of spiritual significance seemed to be lost no matter how skillful the renovations were. What was lost, of course, was the reliability of the "sanctuary."

Critics of a pastoral approach to preaching sometimes misconstrue this to mean that the *content* of preaching has to be excessively introspective, socially myopic, or repetitive. Nothing of the sort: it is the *approach,* not the content, that is at issue, just as in the basic quietness of therapy we may deal with the most momentous and socially important issues that will take a client into realms of action, relationship, and responsibility whose consequences are life-determining. Here, as a last illustration, is a small personal vignette. Not every preacher works this way, but when I myself was serving a congregation I found it absolutely necessary before worship to have at least a few uninterrupted minutes for my own "sanctuary" before taking on worship leadership. I still do. Since the congregation I served was not used to that pattern, it took some deliberate teaching and learning over a period of time before the message got through that their pastor was not going to charge straight from a church school class through the preworship coffee hour and into the pulpit, gown flapping without ever looking back. The tide turned when a couple of retired air force pilots who were prominent in the congregation one day realized that all I was seeking was the same sort of premission gathering of wits and resources that they themselves had insisted on in their flying days. Once I had my sanctuary, I could turn myself to the "real world" and to the (at least for me) intensely involving task of helping create theirs.

The second prominent feature of the therapeutic environment itself has to do with the giving and receiving of responsibility. Time and again clients come for help assuming that in doing so they have thrown in the towel on being able to help themselves. There is sometimes a guiltiness to them, a sense of having been too weak or unskilled or even "bad" to shoulder their own burdens. Now they have to have a therapist do it for them, and that is a painful admission of inadequacy. What I must first do, then, is correct their impression by reassuring them that they and they alone are responsible for their therapy and in fact are going to be doing the real work. My job is to be there reliably and to hear and respond to them with as much interpretative wisdom as I can muster. What they choose to deal with and how, where and when they choose to alter their lives and actions on the basis of what happens in therapy, and even how well or poorly they make use of the time they are paying good money for are all their responsibilities. Therapy is hard work for a client, when it is done well. If anything, by coming for "help" they are wedding themselves to more, not less, involvement in and responsibility for their own destinies than they had before.

Moreover, the message begins to be sent right from the start that if they can take responsibility for the issues we deal with in the therapeutic environment, they can progressively learn to take similar responsibility for the real world in which they live—a world, by the way, that I as therapist will most likely never enter or know much about firsthand. The same sort of thing can happen with pastoral preaching. Obviously, we are talking about a very different thing from the dependency-creating kinds of preaching that do little more than give people a good dose of optimism (or denial, he said with thinly disguised distaste) for hanging on by their fingernails yet another week. No, what we are talking about here is "equipping the saints" for—the only word for it, really—*discipleship*. The idea you sometimes run into that "pastoral" preaching is somewhere over toward the other end of the spectrum from discipleship is simply false, and the comparison to psychotherapy is intended to underline the point.

Yes, there are clients who begin to rely on their therapy as a substitute for responsibility in the real world. Competent therapists quickly spot that and confront it. The exception, however, does not make the rule, in therapy any more than in preaching. This faintly paradoxical combination of qualities seems the same by whatever names we call them: a moratorium space in which to prepare onself for worldly responsibility or a sanctuary in which we equip ourselves to become disciples. When the very environment is adequate to those things, we have come a long way toward accomplishing our tasks.

THE THERAPEUTIC RELATIONSHIP

What Phillips Brooks and later writers such as H. H. Farmer did for our estimation of the role of the preacher in preaching Sigmund Freud and his followers did for psychotherapy. (It is interesting that both kinds of writing were happening at almost exactly the same time in history.) For some reason, though, preaching has sometimes been uneasy if not downright ashamed about the plain fact that who and what the preacher is counts at times as much as what he or she says. If we look at the world of psychotherapy, however, with its quite

similar dynamic, some of the reasons become clear. The therapist enters into a special and at times baffling relationship with
his or her client, and what Freud taught us was simply that the
nature and quality of that relationship matters to the outcome
at least as much, if not far more than, the content of what the
therapist says. For present purposes I want to talk about three
characteristics of it, though of course there are several others
that a full-dress account would deal with. Only the third, by
the way, would I place under the familiar Freudian category of
transference.

Before anything is said, however, we have to note that
what is established between client and therapist is a *real relationship,* even though of a rather peculiar kind. Clients are
forever worrying that their relationship with the therapist is
somehow not the real thing, and therapists are forever having
to remind them that although it is unique and not the sort of
thing one finds in everyday life, the interaction between the two
nevertheless tips the scales as "real." In some ways it is "more
real than real," owing to the sensitive life material that gets
carried along in it. I intend this opening remark to carry both a
warning and a reassurance to preachers: our relationships with
those who receive our preaching, while they may have "real-
world" dimensions outside worship (in other pastoral work,
friendship, church duties, and the like), are for a short time
each week special, unique, and "more real than real," just as
therapists' are with their clients. We err either if we try to
push that fact away or if we are dissatisfied with it and try to
become a "real-time" associate in the pulpit. For homiletics to
try to teach preachers to be more accessibly human in their
preaching—in both content and delivery—is a very good
thing, of course. Artificial stained-glass voices, first-century
rhetoric, and Jehovan pulpit attitudes are as worthy of exter-
mination as cockroaches (though some would say just as durable). But it is possible to take a good thing too far, and I have
heard rather too much emphasis lately on trying to make the
preaching experience a "real-world" kind of human dialogue
or conversation no different in dynamic from what one would

have sitting in a living room, conducting an adult study group, or talking at the dinner table. That is dangerously naive and threatens to overlook the not only special but vitally necessary qualities of what we are here paralleling with the therapeutic relationship. With that said as prologue, we are ready for the three components of that relationship: (1) loaning a stronger sense of reality, (2) the transitional holding experience, and (3) transference and modeling.

I. THE STRONGER SENSE OF REALITY

The phrase "a stronger sense of reality" (whose source I can no longer identify) may strike us as baffling at first, but when unpacked, it comes to symbolize a crucial and often ignored dynamic for both therapy and, as I am arguing, preaching. What it means is basically this: The therapist is not a paragon of mental health, a guru of the affective domain; his or her contribution to the therapeutic process does not come, as some mistakenly believe, from having "been there and back" success- fully, bringing along an accurate road map to well-being that routes us around all the washouts, detours, and chuckholes of life. No, what has happened in the therapist's own therapy and training is the achievement of a certain clarity and honesty about his or her own place and process in the real world. What that gets us is not necessarily more happiness or better func- tioning (though of course we hope for at least some of that) so much as clearer vision of the boundaries of things: where "I" stop and others begin; how much of my conscious experience is really "out there" and how much is the contribution of my own inner history and perception; what constitutes "cause" and "effect" in sequences of events, particularly when the causality is complex or circular. In short, the therapist is no magician but simply relatively better able than others to deal with reality with a minimum of protective screens and buffers. The process is never perfect, of course, and the word "relatively" has to be doubly underscored. The phrase "stronger sense of reality" does not mean that the therapist is better, healthier, nicer, braver, more socially competent, or wiser than anyone else. It *does* mean that he or she is able to look at the way things really are with fewer filters and less blinking, and less fear of being overwhelmed by what we see.

When I speak of "loaning" that sense of reality to people, I mean simply that in the therapeutic relationship some of my sense of reality becomes available to my clients through a sort of confidence or guiding process, much as a trail guide "loans" me a sense of well-being and of knowing the route when left to my own devices I would be scared witless and probably huddled back in the tent. What happens in the therapy is that by borrowing some of the therapist's sense of reality a client is able to make use of it for a while and take some risks of self-perception and self-understanding that might not have been possible otherwise. Later, what was borrowed will be replaced by what has become the client's own. It is fairly common, for instance, for couples in marriage counseling to be able to talk to each other and perhaps fight with each other in the therapy hour in ways they cannot do at home. "Why," they sometimes ask, "can't we do this on our own?" And I reply that doing it on their own is the goal we are aiming for, but for now they need a little protection from the fearfulness of it all, which is what our time together provides. What has happened is that *my* sense of reality—my awareness that they are not going to be destroyed by talking or even fighting, that the world is not going to fall into pieces no matter how painful things may get—has been "loaned" to them. In time, we hope, the loan will not be needed; they will have their own strengthened senses of reality to carry them through, and that is the objective of the whole process.

I want to say two things about that in theological perspective. First, what we have been talking about seems to belong under the category of "servanthood." The servant is a paradoxical figure, giving itself away to other people but somehow not being depleted in the process. Put another way, the servant must be a strong self for the selflessness of servanthood to work. There are neither doormats nor frozen marble statues in the image. The biblical imagery of first becoming last, greatest being least, and losing one's life in order to save it, all points to that dialectical interplay. It is precisely what I mean by "loaning a stronger sense of reality."

Second, we would do well to remind ourselves that this whole phenomenon was at least theoretically part of the Christian's stock in trade long before psychotherapy was invented. We want to affirm, after all, that faith is able to look life—and death—in the face without being destroyed. We want to say that because of faith we do not need quite the same coping devices we otherwise might. A belief in resurrection takes the place of a need for denial of deaths of all shapes and sizes; confidence in forgiveness lets us do a little more without self-justification and rationalization; hope for reconciliation means we can afford to enter relationships with less score keeping, blaming, and fearfulness. The pastoral preacher represents all that. Notice I do not necessarily say we *talk* about it all the time; it is more a matter of embodying it, of letting it determine the brush pattern of our painting, as I said before. Far more than ingenious diagnosis or helpful advice, the representation of a stronger sense of reality is what makes pastoral preaching "work."

Perhaps this is the place for a brief aside about an often vexing dilemma: how can we talk about what we have not experienced? That can be especially troublesome for young preachers whose track records have just begun. The same thing happens with therapists, who sometimes encounter quite explicitly such anguished and angry charges as "You can't possibly understand what's happening to me; you've never been divorced!" Even when we manage to persuade ourselves that having carbon copies of people's experiences is not the necessary qualification for understanding them, the idea still stings. It doesn't have to, though, when we look at our work from the stronger sense of reality perspective. What we are doing as preachers or therapists is *not*, after all, saying, "I've been there and back and I can tell you how it's done." That posture went out of style (I hope) long ago. What we are saying, in effect, is "I can help you look at what *you* are going through from a slightly different vantage point, without quite so much need for self-defense, and maybe together we will see some hope and possibility we hadn't noticed before."

2. TRANSITIONAL HOLDING

A second feature of the therapeutic relationship is what D. W. Winnicott, an influential British child psychoanalyst, called "transitional holding" or the "holding environment," and this too will most likely be a new term to readers.[2] Behind it is a rather complex theory, which we will not have to unpack in great detail here in order to get the mileage we want out of the concept. Basically, Winnicott reminded us of two things: (1) that part of growing up involves a child's making the transition from fantasy world to real world, bridging the gap between magical expectations and the rough-and-tumble of life-as-it-is, and (2) that basically adequate mothering was an irreplaceable essential in the process, characterized in part by appropriate emotional "holding" of the child as the strenuous transitional process is waged.

The transitional process is symbolized and in some ways enabled by transitional objects and phenomena—the famous "security blankets" of life. These objects are not to be taken lightly; indeed, we can smile about them precisely because they once were so important to *all* of us. The transitional object—toy, blanket, thumb, whatever it may be—is a crucial talisman to the child. It represents *both* fantasy and reality, and as such it is a literal, tangible bridge between the two worlds, across which the child can eventually walk. Relinquishing a transitional object when the time is ripe signals a major emotional event in the child's development: it is the rite of passage into the object world.

As you might imagine, all kinds of things can go wrong with this developmental process, and none of us makes the journey completely unscathed. That brings us to therapy itself, which Winnicott and his followers came to see as a kind of transitional experience in its own right, reenacting and repairing many of the vicissitudes of earlier life. The therapeutic experience itself, with its "sanctuary" quality, partakes of both fantasy and real worlds, enabling a person to retrace his or her tracks, so to speak, in service to a more durable transition experience. I would argue that much the same dynamic is to be found in the worship experience, a point tellingly made by cultural anthropologist Victor Turner and to which we return at length in chapter 8. Here is to be found the "in the world but not of it" quality of which the Gospel of John speaks; hardly a more apt phrase could be found to describe the transitional experience. The pastoral preacher is in this sense as much a transitional guide as is the therapist. The experience over which he or she presides is *invested* with a personal significance that most of our worshipers perhaps could not describe but that it is our responsibility as professionals to understand and treat with great care.

What goes on within the framework of this transitional experience is the other of Winnicott's two main points. Just as the mother "held" the child through its transition, so too the therapist represents a "holding" figure to the client—not, of course, in a literal sense. I have my own personal image for that phenomenon, and perhaps it would be useful here. When my children were younger, they would occasionally bring me precious objects to hold for them, perhaps while we were out walking: rocks, interesting sticks, a bird's eggshell. As they have grown older they have begun to give me other things to "hold": the worries of an early teenager, a dream that excited and confused a child just beginning to know what dreams are anyway, stuffed animals from earlier years put away in the attic and rediscovered for a brief flirtation with "the way it used to be," a tearful phone call reporting the beloved guinea pig's death. Holding these things for them is both an important and a delicate operation, as I have learned to my sorrow in the times I botched the job, perhaps by saying without thinking, "What do we need another old rock for anyhow?"

Both as a therapist and as a preacher I simply do the same thing: I hold the precious things my people bring—their histories, fantasies, hopes, relationships, worries, symptoms, all the rest. In the process, of course, I hold *them*, because that is the nature of a transitional object or experience: it carries part of the person himself or herself with it; that is how it does its work. I come more and more to realize that my skillfulness as a therapist does not depend so much on the expertness of my interpretations or the insightfulness of my observations as it does on my reliability as a "holder." The same is true when I preach. Even though here I am doing all the talking, I remind myself that, in effect, I am holding people through their concerns and issues, most of which are unknown to me but which I inevitably touch with what I say. I am convinced that a great deal can be accomplished in preparing pastoral sermons—on whatever definition one uses—by keeping this aspect of the therapeutic relationship in view, never mind for now the array of techniques, strategies, and downright gimmicks we may bring to our craft. It strikes me as what we have talked endlessly about under the rubric of "stewardship." More than that, though our theologies of the Holy Spirit may differ, there is something about the Johannine image of Jesus promising the coming "comforter" that rings true about holding. I myself do not sense the presence of ghosts, holy or otherwise, in either my therapy or my preaching; but I do know firsthand the mysterious beauty and fascination of the transitional experience, and more than once I have remembered Jesus' promise with the warm sense that even while I am holding, I am held.

3. TRANSFERENCE AND MODELING

About transference I will say relatively little, partly because the concept is already well known. This was Freud's attempt to explain the clearly observable phenomenon that his patients seemed to respond to him as though he were someone other than Sigmund Freud. (In time, of course, he recognized that the same thing happens in the other direction, from therapist to client—what we now call *countertransference*.) His deduction has withstood the test of time and the significant modification of other elements of his theory. Clients unconsciously come to regard their therapist as though he or she were some other significant person in their lives—mother, father, lover, sibling, etc. Certain qualities of the real person are "transferred" over to the therapist, and of course the process is almost entirely out of awareness until it is interpreted by the therapist. The popular cartoon image of people falling in love with their therapists comes from this general idea, though grossly distorted. It is not the therapist exactly who is the recipient of transferential feelings, but whomsoever the therapist comes to represent; and it may just as easily be anger, fear, or any other feeling as love (much to the discomfort of all of us, who along with the rest of the population would rather be loved than abused).

What Freud first regarded as a nuisance that interfered with analysis quickly came to be seen as a vital part of the psychoanalytic process. By projecting attributes of signficant others onto the therapist, a client was able in the safe environment of therapy to relive and perhaps relearn certain aspects of previously troubled experience and relationship. The therapeutic hour became a kind of testing laboratory, and the transference was the experimental product. Or, as it came to be said among therapists, it is the transference (to other people) that makes people sick, and it is the transference (to the therapist) that cures. Feelings and behaviors that were formerly locked up, so to speak, inside the person could gradually be unlocked and then dealt with through the transferential phenomenon, so that they no longer plagued the person's functioning through their unconscious, but still potent, influence.

A related aspect of the therapeutic alliance we could call *modeling,* though such a term does not have nearly the acceptance and stature that *transference* does. I believe, though, that modeling is an essential ingredient in the whole transferential cycle. In essence what happens is that the therapist, now in the role of some other person to the client, behaves quite differently than that other person would. The therapist holds out the possibility, "models" it, we could say, that the interaction that is being rehearsed in the therapy need not stay in the same troublesome ruts it has been in for the client. So, for instance, if a client is seeing me in the role of father and gets angry at me (but not really at me so much as at the father I represent) *but* I do not respond with the brutal retaliation or cutting put-down or whimpering collapse or whatever the reaction of the real father was, then I have, in effect, modeled for the client a very different kind of interaction with a person of such significance as a father might have. It offers the client a chance to "play it again" but with a different outcome, and in that process growth and change may take place. A lot of therapy comes down to a process of relearning old things with more adequate models.

Though it may seem farfetched at first, this aspect of the therapeutic alliance has a strong parallel in pastoral preaching, even though we are sometimes afraid of it. For one thing, the dynamics of transference are found in nontherapeutic interactions (though perhaps less intensely) whenever issues of heavily freighted personal significance are involved—the very sort of situation you will find in pastoral preaching. Thomas Oden long ago observed that the nonjudgmental love and acceptance of the counselor represented in tangible form the very *sort* of love that God offers us—through an analogical, modeling process.[3] Why, one might wonder, would such a potent phenomenon automatically stop when the same pastor puts on a robe and climbs into the pulpit? The answer is simple: it would not and does not.

Let me offer a small example. In a recent pastoral preaching course I assigned the task of preparing short sermons directly on a variety of pastoral topics—depression, grief, moving, interpersonal conflict, and the like. After in-class discussion and revision, some of the sermons were actually preached in the students' field education churches. One after another reported almost identical reactions from the listening congregations: they were surprised and relieved even to hear such topics addressed from the pulpit, and the fact that the preachers were not afraid to face these issues, even in the absence of clear answers or solutions, itself sent a strong message of encouragement that the people could themselves do likewise. What was happening was simply that in the bare act of lifting up difficult issues often swept under the chancel carpet, the preachers were *modeling* a kind of courage and confidence that Christian faith had something directly to do with such things. No, I am not arguing that all those people "saw" in these student preachers images of their parents, siblings, spouses, and all the rest. I *am* suggesting, however, that by dint of his or her traditionally vested authority in the pulpit, if nothing else, the preacher becomes a more-than-usually-significant figure for people when highly invested matters are talked about. That is certainly a transferential reaction, and the modeling that goes with it of a posture or approach or way of dealing with those matters carries just as much message value in the pulpit as it does in the counseling room.

When we search for a theological expression of the whole phenomenon, we come upon something I am almost hesitant to identify. Try as I will, however, I cannot quite get away from it: something very like this process seems to be gathered up in the concept of *atonement*. I am not thinking so much here of the *doctrine* of the Atonement, with its complicated and controversial variations and developments, as of the general image and concept itself: the idea that in some way human beings are placed in a different relationship with God because Jesus takes onto himself and transforms some of our own quality of being. The transferential relationship is, in that sense, on the order of an "atoning" one in terms of its underlying human dynamics. Something about the way God's love works is proclaimed in the process, and that, of course (in a roundabout way), is the concern of this chapter.

THERAPEUTIC OBJECTIVES

The last base we want to touch in this section on the functions of psychotherapy and pastoral preaching is the question of what exactly we aim to accomplish in the processes. Here I want to be more explicitly theological and to argue more directly that the fruits of the pastoral process and the content of our "proclamation" are one and the same thing, expressed through different language in different contexts. A list of objectives in the therapeutic process could get very long indeed. I have selected five that seem most central. Here the parallels to preaching are more obvious and I will say less about that side of things. The main thing is to realize how what in some sense are already familiar objectives in preaching are at the same time the aims of therapeutic communication. It is that convergence I am trying to illustrate and make a case for throughout this chapter.

The first objective is the *learning of limits and consequences,* something which in theological terms we might well call *discipline* (understanding, of course, a nonpunitive use of the term). There is a sense, it is true, in which people come to therapy in the first place because they have run smack into their limits and been bruised by the process. Surprisingly, though, that message often seems not to have gotten through. What needs to happen is something like the custom in New England of walking the boundaries of a piece of land you are going to buy. Because the parcels are often irregular and the deeds ancient, a wise buyer, I am told, physically treks along the property line to get a firsthand, visual sense of what the purchase really involves. In therapy we slowly walk along the boundaries of a person's past experience, identity, capabilities, and aspirations so that he or she can get a firsthand sense of what is there—and, more important sometimes, *not* there. Only then can we set ourselves to the task of changing those limits, within whatever scope is possible.

The same sort of thing can be said about consequences. Few of us, I think, are able to envision with any regularity the consequences on down the line of most of the things we do. At our best we will be able to anticipate a few links of the chain, and at our worst, of course, we blunder through life with utterly no knowledge of or regard for the consequences. When we put that into past tense, most of us are only dimly aware of the consequences that have already happened to us as a result of what we have experienced. Again and again clients are surprised to discover how past experiences have impacted and influenced who they are now. Both forward and backward we must go in therapy, gradually learning how things are connected, in the hope that from now on we will be relatively less buffeted about by events or feelings we had little comprehesion of before, and also relatively better able to take responsibility for the consequences of what we do.

A second objective is *learning how to manage conflict,* both internal and external, both past and present. Conflict theory has a central place in many understandings of communication, personality development, social interaction, and psychotherapy. The phenomenon of unresolved conflict was central to Freud's own work and understanding. The theological "home" for this dimension of things strikes me as confession. In confession we come to an acknowledgment of much of our basic conflictedness—the things undone we ought to have done, and done we ought not to have done, as Paul says—as an inescapable part of the human condition. There are some basic "axes" of conflict: between ourselves and other selves; between ourselves and the "not-self," or death; between ourselves as finite creatures and ultimate reality, or God. Conflict is the precondition both of neurosis and of creativity, depending on how we wage it. Learning to wage it better and more creatively is what we are after in the therapeutic endeavor. That involves preeminently (whether we use the theological language or not) a posture of "confession," of getting in touch with painful things that have happened both to us and by our own hands, in order that we might be set free to live on different and larger trajectories.

Clarifying and restructuring relationships is a third objective of therapy, and it is easy enough to see that through theological lenses as *reconciliation*. I would add only one note: reconciliation too often carries with it the connotation of the peaceful, happy ending, and life does not always work out that way—nor should it. With clarifying and restructuring we achieve a more realistic, honest, and open way of being-in-relationship, even when that *may* mean such nonpacific outcomes as agreeing to disagree, or severing a living arrangement, or facing the impossibility of making someone different, or taking a firmly oppositional stand to something or someone. Those things, too, I would want to call "reconciliation." The key thing is learning not to fool ourselves or operate on false assumptions.

For example, a young woman comes for help because she is unable to form any lasting relationships with men and seems tied to her parents. She was the "problem child" of the family growing up and continues to do a fairly complete job of messing up her work, her social friendships, her career plans, and her interactions with parents and siblings. What comes out during her treatment is a sad and familiar pattern. She was unconsciously "chosen" in her family as the one-with-the-problems, and by continually focusing on how badly she was doing things, from childhood on, the family (especially the parents) was conveniently distracted from their own miserable relationships and failure. Clarifying and restructuring relationships for this woman means, among other things, coming to a recognition of the role she has played all these years without knowing it, particularly with respect to her parents, whom she lets keep her on a very short and tight emotional leash—even now that she is a fully independent adult. It would be nice to think that reconciliation could mean that her parents also will come to an understanding of what has been going on all these years, so that everyone can change their relative positions. Unhappily, in this case (though by no means in all) that is impossible. The parents are too old, too resistant, and too caught up in their own agonies even to be approachable. Reconciliation for this woman means a recognition that she is never going to be able to please her parents as all children want to and that if she is to have a lasting and fulfilling relationship with a man it is going to be at the price of her bondage to her parents' whims and wishes. *Some* kind of *modus vivendi* can be achieved, but it simply will not be accompanied by grateful tears of relief and the violins coming up at the end.

A fourth objective is really rather global but bears mentioning explicitly: *broadening a person's permissible range of experience and feeling*. We want our clients to be able to reach out for more of life and not have to limit themselves unduly behind barricades of self-protection, fear, guilt, calculatedness, or what have you. I would call that "having the mind of Christ," at the risk of raising the ire of some theological friends for whom it will not seem nearly "religious" enough. Again and again, however, what strikes us about the outlook of Jesus in the New Testament is simply its courageous freedom to *take in everything it encounters*. One of the main dramatic themes of the narrative parts of the gospels is Jesus' associates' repeated attempts to impose on Jesus himself their own limitations on what they are able to experience. Again and again we find them trying to keep him out of uncomfortable personal situations, away from bothersome details, or within the confines of social and legal decency. There is a rather nice literary sense, I think, in which Jesus removes the "fence" of the Torah and frees both people and the law to range more widely through the created order—including its limitations and its muck. It takes a certain kind of "mind" to achieve that freedom, that perspective. It takes a mind that is thoroughly at home with its creatureliness because it looks at it from the perspective of ultimacy. It takes a mind that can risk seeing beyond the obvious because it believes nothing is exempt from God's care. It takes a mind that does not have to calculate and cajole about relationships because it has no fear either of being rejected or of doing harm.

If something like that is the "mind of Christ," then having something closer to it is what we are trying for in both the therapeutic process and in pastoral preaching. Therapy is "successful" not when its recipients get all their problems solved and everything is happy—that is not going to happen completely for anyone, ever, this side of the eschaton. No, therapy has "worked" in large measure when people are better able than they were to open themselves to more of what the real world offers in experience and feeling and are not overwhelmed or destroyed but able to respond humbly and creatively.

The final objective I would mention is caught very well by the biblical image of "freeing the captives": *for people to be free to make the choices and decisions of living*. Some degree of volitional paralysis gets to all of us, at least under certain circumstances. We may respond in those times either by retreating into nondecision and letting life just wash over us or by flinging out wildly with what seem to be "choices" but are really little more than the orbital thrusts of random drivenness. We are captive to our fears, our ignorance, our prejudices, our unhealed wounds, our unresolved conflicts, and our ill-chosen values. A mistaken popular stereotype of therapy is that it produces self-serving hedonists who are "free" to romp through life getting their own needs met and damn both the consequences and the neighbors. Whatever else that may be, it is not "freedom" in either a theological or a responsible therapeutic sense.

All five of these objectives apply with little or no translation to pastoral preaching. I will close this chapter with just one more statement of its basic point. While there are certainly times and places for appropriate theological talk, it is short-sighted to limit what we mean by "proclamation of the gospel" to theological *content*. As a committed Christian, I of course hope that people will be able to use and grow from the traditional symbols of the faith, with their rich, dialectical significance. If anything, however, I am even more hopeful that they will be able to live out this "gospel," whether or not they would recognize it in print. Pastoral preaching is dedicated to achieving a balance between the life experience and the articulated interpretation because they interact and interpenetrate. Making that plain and creating environments in which it can happen is what the pastoral preaching ministry is about.

With this perspective on proclamation in hand, we now must turn to the highly specialized communication environment of preaching, to do some mapping of what I will call the communicative field.

5. Mapping the Communicative Field

Most of us think of preaching as more or less a cause-and-effect operation. We say something that causes listeners to react in a certain way; listeners do something (like squirming or staring at us with breathless, rapt attention) that causes us to deliver our message one way but not another. Earlier, we had prepared our sermons on the same basis: certain things in our daily experience or reading or personal agendas caused us to set down the words and ideas of a sermon in some fashion that would have been different had the antecedent factors differed. We link "causes" with communicative "effects."

While that is not a bad working metaphor, it is not sufficient either, particularly for understanding pastoral preaching. It is too simple, too "straight-line," too unforgiving of those subtleties of the communicative situation that may, in the end, count for more than the identifiable "causes." A better, though admittedly more cumbersome, way to look at things is through the idea of a *communicative field*. By *field* I simply mean the whole array of conscious and unconscious forces at work in a given communication situation that make it what it uniquely is: assumptions, felt needs, available information, the current social and historical setting, data presented to the field by messages, language usage, the physical setting, and so on through a potentially very long list of things. In other words, instead of trying to gauge the work of a sermon by looking at what factors cause which effects, we can look instead to the total interacting field of forces, thereby taking into account many things that straight-line causal thinking would miss.

The idea of a field of anything is, of course, a common and very broad-gauged metaphor; there are dozens of things it can mean, as elaborations of its basic underlying idea. For our purposes in talking about pastoral preaching, however, I want to look at two uses of the idea: one as a way of talking about different types of communication and the other as a way of seeing how the same basic information can, when placed in different fields, create very different outcomes in terms of how its recipients perceive themselves and respond as a community of faith.

THE COMMUNICATIVE FIELDS

The idea of a communicative field is based on some working assumptions. They are not overly complicated, but they are not always overly explicit either, which is why it will pay to list some of them at the outset.

1. Most basically, we are talking about *a field of interaction* with many forces operating in many directions at once—the preacher's, the people's, the setting's, the *absent* participants', and so on. Finding Cause A to match with Effect B is largely fruitless, because the directions of influence of these forces go every which way for *all* participants. We brace ourselves, in other words, for a complex picture that is never going to be as complete as our cause-and-effect thinking would really like.

2. We are talking about *relationships within the field,* relationships that existed before the sermon, are affected by it, and will continue after the preaching is over. That these relationships exert a profound influence on how information is received and processed is something it will not hurt to remind working preachers. We sometimes tend to overrate the power of what we say to stand on its own, as though the interation between preacher and people—or among the people themselves—had less influence even on simple, straightforward comprehension (let alone the interpretation of meaning) than it in fact does.

3. We are talking about *more than ordinary concerns,* though in a context of mundane experiences, forces, values, and relationships. It was Barth who commented that while the Bible should be read alongside the morning newspaper, the fact was that the

Bible did not concern itself with ordinary matters. No, it was occupied by the "boundary conditions," so to speak, the times and places in human experience when even everyday things became somehow momentous and life-determining. The anticipation of dealing with *extra*ordinary matters is an assumption of the communicative field of preaching.

4. *Language is a two-edged sword:* it may serve to create and clarify meaning, thereby facilitating communication, but it may also serve—however unwittingly—to confuse meaning and block communication. The old bromide about what you mean being blocked by what you say is really quite apt, when you get down to it. We preachers tend to work on the assumption that the worst breakdown of our language happens when it fails to get across what we want it to. Not so. The worst is when it blocks and cancels out communication.

5. *No communicative field is wholly positive or wholly negative.* They all contain both negative elements of anxiety and resistance and positive elements of success and celebration. As a communicator I must keep in mind the fact that no matter how good or bad the field appears overall, the disparate elements are there and at work. That is why, after all, we can make the twin theological assertions that no successful human work is without its "sinfulness" and that no seemingly hopeless situation is beyond the power of God's redemption.

6. *The preacher brings a set of assumptions to the field* about how people are going to respond to what he or she says. They might include such things as these: listeners will see themselves in the sermon; biblical ideas, experiences, and roles are relevant to these people today; listeners are open to challenge and correction; listeners are receptive of comfort and reassurance; people will believe what I say. Of course the assumptions may be very different—even disastrously so, as with a preacher who assumes without quite realizing it that no one is going to believe the sermon, that the people are a stiff-necked bunch out to get him, and that they were not really worth bothering about in the first place. Moral to the story: to understand the field, we have to get in touch with our own working assumptions.

7. *Listeners also bring their corresponding assumptions,* which might include the following: the preacher wants to say something directly relevant to my life; the biblical material of the sermon will have something to do with me; I may be challenged or corrected or confronted with my inadequacies and failings; I may find what the preacher says comforting or supportive; the preacher will tell the truth. Of course, here, too, I have described the kind of listener we all want to preach to; real life may not be quite so accommodating!

8. *The field created in, by, and for the preaching acts as a "container" for these assumptions and the personal investments underlying them.* The degree to which positive and helpful communication occurs depends in large part upon the type of field created and how well it "holds" what participants bring to it. Here is the same idea of "holding" we encountered earlier. It is important to realize (as we are about to discuss in more detail) that different *types* of communicative field differ in what they are able to "contain." If the preacher is working on the basis of one type while the people are in another, spillage is going to occur and some degree of confusion, anxiety, and miscommunication is going to result.

9. *Time, both past and future, is an essential part of the communicative field.* We bring our previous experiences to it as well as our future expectations. A preacher just beginning a pastoral relationship will be acutely aware of the time dimension as he or she wonders what sort of communicative experience the people are accustomed to, what they respond well or badly to, what they need and expect, and all the rest. All too often we make the mistake of assuming that a new preaching ministry or a new sermon wipes the slate clean and that people are ready to start fresh. Such a willingness may be there, all right, but it has a field context that is bound to include past and future. We ignore it at our peril.

That, then, is the general idea, and I think you will find it essential to talking about restoration as our orienting purpose in pastoral preaching. We are moving away from what you could call a "problem-solving" or "personal fix-up" approach. When we think of restoration, as a matter of fact, we are dealing with fields of personal functioning and self-understanding; it is a far more wholistic idea than just working with this or that knotty problem or vexing issue. The restorer pays attention to subtle interconnections and influences in what he or she is working on. Making a change over in this corner affects the total effort far more than those limited things that are directly and causally connected to the particular move. Without a sensitivity to the overall field, restoration becomes, you could say, "redecoration," sometimes with disastrous results!

With that general orientation to the field-of-forces metaphor in hand, let us turn now to the two more particular uses of the idea promised earlier in this chapter: as type of communication and as receiver self-perception.

TYPES OF COMMUNICATION

A large number of investigators interested in human communication have noticed (and variously identified) the phenomenon that we commonly think, experience, and communicate in two different ways. Perhaps the most popular recent description of that duality is the now common distinction between "right brain" and "left brain" activity, the former referring to a more imaginal, creative, and interior way of thinking and the latter suggesting a more rational, problem-solving, and real-world process. The underlying idea itself, however, has a long history. Bruce Reed summarizes several major theoretical positions on the subject, while contributing his own terminology of "S-activity" and "W-activity" to denote the two strands.[1]

For our purposes, the impact of that thinking is to describe two very different communicative fields, and we will draw from an analysis of therapeutic communication made by Robert Langs, a creative and highly regarded psychoanalyst.[2] Since throughout this book we are making use of a rough analogy to psychotherapy, this approach fits the scheme of things. Unlike

Reed and others he summarizes, Langs speaks of three basic types of communication each of which defines a certain field of interaction among its participants, the third situation being not so much a field itself as the breakdown of the other two. The *behavior* of those involved as well as the *usefulness* of the experience depend in large measure on how the field is structured by the different communication types or styles. As you will shortly see, the first two types are both productive, though in very different ways, while the third is basically destructive of what the therapist, and by analogy the pastoral preacher, is trying to achieve. Rather than Langs's rather unpoetic "A," "B," and "C," we will call them symbolic, action-discharge, and disengaged fields.

The Symbolic Field

Langs calls this simply the "Type A field," but "symbolic" is in fact what it is; Reed calls it "S-activity." The communication of the symbolic field is dominantly metaphoric, a conjunction of real and not real so that participants emerge more real than before in their living. This is the transitional space between hard-nosed reality and imagined possibility. In it we recognize that the language we use has that special quality Paul Ricoeur calls "semantic impertinence" to describe how metaphors both participate in the reality of what they represent and push beyond it.[3] Our biblical and theological images are at home here: the kingdom of God, living water, the tree bearing fruit, and hundreds more.

The function of symbolic communication is the interpretation of both contents and mechanisms of thought by eliciting them in and referring them to the field of interaction. The symbolic language holds and carries my thought and my life processes, letting me perceive them in new lights, allowing me to get closer to them just as in play we get closer to things we would have to back away from in "real life." (Children "playing dead," grown-ups reading Stephen King horror stories, and worshipers listening to a sermon on the raising of Lazarus are all doing the same kind of thing in terms of the symbolic field of communication.)

Symbolic communication results both in more insight and also in more intense experience of what is in my thought and feeling. As with any metaphoric interaction, this kind of communication involves us in some degree of temporary mental disorganization. That is, we are not in the comfortable world of straight descriptions of things-as-they-are but in the more transitional domain of what-might-be. Because of that inner dynamic there will inevitably be some degree of anxiety and resistance to the sheer fact that the communicative ground we stand on is not nearly as firm or predictable as, say, a lecture on the history of the Bible. But there is also more celebration and more affirmation of a different sense of the real world than we otherwise had. Growth, we are reminded in this field of interaction, is always a process of the disintegration of the status quo, an excursion through uncertainty, and the reintegration of things in a newer and better way.

Perhaps the experience of reading or hearing a poem is as good an illustration as any of what the symbolic communicative field is like. For a short time I relinquish my traditionally literal grasp of something and let myself be guided by the poem. What I am reading both is and is not a description of what it purports to be; it is a metaphor. To "join" it costs me something of the comfort of familiarity and predictability, but at the same time it rewards me with a new perspective, with the exhilaration of seeing something—including myself—from a different vantage point. Who and what I am vis-à-vis this real world is different; I am free to imagine what it is like on "the road less travelled," and perhaps I will be free in the future actually to find myself there.

In therapy symbolic communication is concerned with images, dreams, associations, and the symbolic meanings of both thoughts and actions. In pastoral preaching it deals sometimes with those same kinds of things, but the hallmark of the symbolic field is this sense of what we might call "active suspendedness" between the literal-descriptive and the conceivable-interpretative—or, if you will, between reality and fantasy.

The Action-Discharge Field

The dominant feature of this second field of communication is not symbol and metaphor but rather a here-and-now, literal quality of the present experience itself. Reed calls it "W-activity," standing for "work." In it we recognize qualities of our*selves* that emerge and are projected, so to speak, onto the message and the communicator. If the symbolic field was characterized primarily by a certain kind of thinking, the action-discharge field is made up primarily of feelings stimulated by the communication itself but intimately related to what I as participant brought to the field to begin with. So, for instance, my insecurity over the future becomes an expectation that the preacher and the message will let me feel that in the end all will be well. The insecurity emerges and is projected onto communicator and message. Or my anger at authority may become a resistance to a preacher's telling me how to live my life. My feeling of lack of nurture translates into a hope (or a demand) that the preacher and the sermon take care of me and allow me to feel sustained. My obscured identity is discharged in this field as a hope that I will be made special before God and these people.

The examples I have used are troublesome, difficult feelings, and that is precisely the point: what in more usual circumstances I would rather not recognize in myself is uncovered here and "held" or contained in the preaching event. It is not an easy experience, either for congregation or for preacher. Bion's list of four essential qualities for a psychoanalyst can easily be transferred over to the pastoral preacher in the action-discharge field.[4] First, the preacher must be able to provide nurturance, permission, and assurance that the feelings we are having will not overwhelm or destroy us, that it is possible to act and feel as we do before God without being struck down. Second, the preacher must be able to maintain a "state of reverie," that is, a mood and posture where emotion and reflection can have free play while the reality consequences are temporarily suspended. (I can feel my anger, for instance, in the confidence that I am not in fact going to throttle my neighbor right this minute.) Third, the preacher must be able to think symbolically, that is, to offer a model of the work of language as mediating reality indirectly, so that we are assured that *saying* something does not *cause* it to be so. Fourth, the preacher must be able to receive listeners' projections and represent a transformation of them via the symbolic process, so that my picture of myself does not become an enactment of what I immediately feel.

Those four capabilities are essential to pastoral preaching: providing nurturance, maintaining a state of possibility, guiding symbolic thinking, and receiving listeners' projections. They define what it means to "hold" or "contain" the people and the process of this kind of communication.

The Disengaged Field

With the third communicative field we must make a careful distinction, because in some ways it *looks* like ordinary, informational communication, the kind we probably spend most of our time doing, and necessarily so. What we are describing, though, as the disengaged field is not nearly so benign: it is the kind of communication that blocks and neutralizes the dynamics of the symbolic and action-discharge fields. So far as pastoral preaching goes, it is the enemy. Langs himself uses the terms "stasis/noncommunication/defense" to describe it, and that title alone should alert us to its seriousness.

Here we find a strong emphasis on the flatly literal manifest content of things, never mind either metaphor or feeling. (Here, too, arises the danger of confusion with other informational communication. It is important to keep in mind the *purpose* and *context* of either therapy or pastoral preaching: to deal with personally invested issues that simply cannot be reached by straight, disengaged "information." Though it is a subtle distinction, we do nevertheless have to say that what is a "disengaged" communicative field in the setting, let us say, of a sermon about grief might be appropriate informational communication in some other setting.) Language is working as a defense against the threat of inner disorganization and challenge (which, as we saw, is always present in the other two fields, necessarily so for them to do their communicative work). In the disengaged field, barriers, falsifications, and emotional "lies" predominate. Let me give two examples, one from a therapeutic setting and a second from preaching itself.

A client in the early stages of his therapy was chronically late for appointments, for the superficially sensible "reason" that he had to drive a fair distance to keep them and was forever getting involved in traffic delays or route changes (the real reason, of course, being resistance to the treatment itself). On one occasion he arrived late as usual and parked his car in a restricted area reserved (because of a legal requirement concerning zoning ordinances) for a few counseling service staff vehicles. When I reminded him that he was not permitted to park there, he began a long and tedious argument about "rights," the "injustice" of such a parking regulation, and my intellectual cowardice in not being willing to "debate" him on the matter. This rather remarkable display of obfuscation went on to the extent that it threatened to consume what was left of the entire counseling hour—which, of course, was its whole unconscious purpose. It was an effort to disengage from the kind of communication that was unsettling to him, and in this case it took the form of an attack on the therapist, carefully clothed in highly rational and literal-minded discourse. Had we been two staff members in an administrative committee meeting trying to work out an equitable system of parking regulations, it might have been appropriate (though minus the telltale emotional coloration of defensiveness and avoidance). Here, however, it was purely disruptive; its purpose was the destruction of the possible meaning of either symbolic or action-discharge fields, which were what the context called for.

A second example from preaching itself, this time involving the primary communicator: in the midst of an otherwise helpfully pastoral sermon on depression in the context of Christian hope, a preacher unaccountably veered off into a highly technical and abstract discussion of a form-critical problem in the biblical text, followed by an equally remote exhortation about how Christians "must" believe this and that in order to ward off trouble. The emotional and symbolic involvement in the topic was effectively short-circuited by the switch to the disengaged field of communication. (The same thing happens on the receiver's end when, for example, my mind wanders away from what is being said—assuming that it is otherwise interesting and pure boredom has not set in—and begins to concentrate on utterly irrelevant things, gets annoyed with the preacher himself or herself for this or that trivial reason, or locks onto a particular fragment of something said and gnaws it like a bone. All are ways of disengaging.)

I believe it has to be said, though with some caution, that several familiar problems with preaching are actually the disengaged communicative field at work. Some strongly "confrontational" preaching would fall into this category. It has also been one of the fatal flaws of much social-action preaching that falls on deaf ears—because, in effect, the approach is an invitation to *dis*engagement rather than to involvement. Preaching that seems to consist of the repetition of familiar and safe theological code phrases, or that again and again worries about irrelevant issues, or that seems to carry a covert plea for acceptance of the preacher, or that tends to violate our expectations by running overtime or being needlessly combative—all are candidates for a diagnosis of "disengaged communicative field."

Pastoral preaching is hard work. The best summary I could give of this section is a quotation from Robert Langs himself, who, though talking about the analyst, could as easily be talking about the pastor:

In addition to being capable of symbolic communication, an analyst must be able to tolerate the anxiety and dread related to experiencing the intensely primitive and horrifying inner mental world of these patients and to the threats to his own defenses against surprisingly similar inner contents. He must also analyze and resolve his dread of containing his patient's underlying destructive, projective identification and his fear of being driven crazy by the patient. . . . He must master his dread of being attacked and even annihilated by the patient's noncommunication and negative projective identifications, which create a void in which his capacity to think, formulate, organize—to function meaningfully and relatedly—are being destroyed by the patient's Type C [disengaged] style.[5]

COMMUNITIES IN THE MAKING

A second way of getting at the idea of a communicative field is to look not at types of communication as we just did but rather at how different combinations of relationships, needs, and interactions create different listening publics or communities. What will be created by a given sermon—or, more likely, by a longer term of preaching—is partly within the control of the preacher. By knowing something about the options we can begin to be more strategic and more intentional in planning our pastoral preaching.

The basic idea here is that *messages create communities,* or, as it is sometimes said in communication jargon, publics. To receive a certain message intelligibly and meaningfully, I as a listener must adopt a certain mental and social posture, almost like imagining myself the kind of person and in the kind of audience that the message was designed *for.* We commonly speak of the need for a communicator to take the role of his or her hearers in order to understand "where they are" and design the message to fit their receptivity. The same process works from the other end as well: a listener willy-nilly puts himself or herself into a certain role in order to understand the communicator. If I am listening to a recital of Robert Frost's poetry, for example, I adopt a certain attitude and self-awareness in order to be as fully open to it as I can. I relax my literal temper to some degree, give myself credit for being able to comprehend complex metaphors and rhythms of language, and let myself be open to receiving what is offered as a gift, so to speak, to my perception. If, on the other hand, the communicative occasion is an administrative staff meeting in the institution where I work and the president begins to reprimand us for slovenly performance and public incivility, I adopt a very different posture: I become acutely aware of lines of authority, to some degree I brace myself either for self-protection or (if I'm one of the culprits) for punishment, and I begin to think of myself as in the spotlight for examination. In either case, since I am surrounded by other people, I comprehend the message by turning myself, chameleonlike, into the kind of person I perceive the message is beamed toward. In effect, I inwardly answer a simple but profound question: "Who must I be to be hearing this message and responding this way?"

Of course, I always have the option of checking out of the process altogether and deciding that this message simply is not for me. I may stop attending to it, or perhaps I will create for myself the posture of an outside observer of all those other people who are a certain kind of public, or perhaps I will even distort how I hear the message so that I make it fit more comfortably the image of what public I choose to be in at the moment. Whichever option I take, however, I am still involved with the business of being a member of one kind of community or another, created in and through the communication process as the way we basically comprehend messages.

With that idea in place, we have a powerful tool for looking at the communicative field of preaching: it can be thought of as the sort of community that comes into being under the influence of a particular message, communicative style, or long-term preaching strategy. Each sermon has behind it an assumption (perhaps unstated or unconscious) about what kind of community it really is intended for. It is the nature of the communication process that to one degree or another, depending on the skillfulness of the communicator, that sermon with its attached assumption will in fact turn its hearers momentarily into just that kind of group.

There are two morals to that story. One is that it pays preachers to find out what their assumptions in fact are for sermons, lest the community they create turns out to be very different from what they thought they wanted. The other is that a large part of the pastoral work of preaching consists not so much in what is said as in the kind of community that is structured. That is a powerful dynamic and working tool, far more important than any technical expertise we might covet in the handy hints and ardent advice department. Our pastoral work and wisdom, in other words, rests at least as much on this field-structuring dynamic as it does on the cleverness or profundity of what we say (though, of course, the two are intertwined).

To illustrate how all that works I want to do a little experiment. Let us take a simple theological assertion and, keeping the information itself as constant as possible, see how by handling it in different ways we create very different communities in the communicative field. In this case I want to use ten different biblical texts, each of which contains essentially the same actual information, viz., that Jesus Christ, as Son of God, is the sovereign Lord. In other words, regardless of which text we preached on, we would be dealing with fundamentally the same underlying theological idea, the lordship of Christ. Then let us see, however, how very *different* the net effect of those texts as messages would be from the perspective of their community-building dynamic. In other words, we will get a glimpse of the idea of the communicative field at work.

Obviously, each of these texts (or, more correctly, the complete pericope that would no doubt be the text for actual preaching purposes) allows different kinds of developments. I am by no means proposing a "right" or "complete" interpretation here, only trying to see how the basic thrust of each text creates a different communicative field, *even though the informational content is in each case fundamentally the same.*

1. " . . . *every tongue confess that Jesus Christ is Lord, to the glory of God the Father" (Phil. 2:11)*. This ancient and beautiful christological hymn, though full of strong feeling and devotion, nevertheless displays a posture of confident belief and rationality. One who says or sings or hears it senses an alignment with a secure community, in which at least in this moment the ambiguities, struggles, and uncertainties yield to a sense of togetherness and solidity. To hear this message and participate fully in it I see myself as a member of what I would call *the established community* (making no apology for the adjective, which in some circles has gotten a bad press).

2. *"Even so, come Lord Jesus" (Rev. 22:20).* Here, of course, is the penultimate word of the New Testament, also carrying as its basic information an affirmation of the lordship of Jesus Christ. The posture I take as a listener, however, is very different from before. Now I find myself in the dominant field of waiting—for fulfillment, for disclosure, for comfort, for challenge, for the promises of the kingdom evoked all in a moment by that single plea of Christian hope down through the centuries, "Maranatha!" It is a hopeful message, to be sure, but it is uttered under the clearly felt pressure of living in an in-between time. This is the testimony of *the waiting community*.

3. *"Lord have mercy on us, Son of David!" (Matt. 20:31)* This plea of two blind beggars on the road to Jerusalem is echoed again and again in similar New Testament encounters with people "on the outside," yearning (and half-fearing) to be healed. Interpreters often note that even in the midst of skepticism and illness these people make an affirmation of faith—which is what Jesus responds to. The posture of the message is plainly that of need and despair. There is only minimal reason for confidence, though some shred of hope remains. The most visible thing is that one who speaks thus recognizes that he or she is an outsider, on the margins of society far from the mainstream of life or religion. In this communicative field, still cluthing the basic, though now almost threadbare, affirmation of Christ's lordship, I am a member of *the marginal community*.

4. *"Are you he who is to come, or shall we look for another?"* *(Luke 7:19)* The feeling now is strikingly different in the words John's disciples use to query Jesus. Here is virtually what the later church would call "anxious inquiry," the peculiar combination of doubt, hope, and fearfulness that creates what we could call *the searching community.* To be sure, there are elements of search and inquiry in some of the other fields as well, but this one simply *seems* different—and so it is. When I stand in it I clearly hope that the answer to the question uttered will be "Yes," but I am not clinging to that hope as desperately as when I am a member of the marginal community or as confidently as when I belong to the established one. There is an almost astringent quality here, the same thing you find in some forms of tightly controlled anxiety.

5. *"You are the Christ, the Son of the living God"* *(Matt. 16:16).* With Peter's confession the mood abruptly changes. Here is the posture of personal confession in a context of discovery, almost of excitement. The whole text (particularly Jesus' response to Peter) makes it abundantly clear, of course, that this is very much an "in-process" faith being expressed. It will be sorely tested; the discovery will have to be verified as painfully and repetitively as any such disclosure inevitably must be. But with all that still to come, it is nevertheless clear that when I hear and respond to the message of this text I am a member of *the confessing community.* I choose that word carefully and mean it to convey the traditional dialectic of Christian "confession," that interplay of belief and process that is never wholly intellectual even though it is expressed rationally, never completely certain despite its fundamental confidence, and above all never smug.

6. *"I believe; help my unbelief!"* *(Mark 9:24)* I find it interesting that when this famous verse is quoted orally it often comes out *"Lord, I believe. . . ,"* even though the address to Jesus is not really there, no doubt because it is clear from the context that at least some part of an affirmation of Jesus' lordship is present. There is, though, almost an impatience to the man's cry, not so much with Jesus as with the whole idea, let us say, of orthodoxy.

This is the posture of devout skepticism that, however, is asking for help rather than indoctrination. It acknowledges that its belief is not complete but begs that whatever faith it has be taken as at least sufficient for Jesus' response. This is the voice of *the outside community*—not marginal as before, because it is clear that the man is a member of "the crowd," the mainstream of people, rather than a beggar or blind one beside the road. But it is outside the ranks of those whose belief is complete, the orthodox.

7. *"We had hoped he was the one"* (Luke 24:21). The mood of Emmaus is gathered up in this small fragment: we had hoped, but it is now three days. . . . Here, without fanfare, is the voice of *the betrayed community,* of those who feel themselves abandoned despite the height of their spirits only days ago. If I truly hear the message of this text, truly participate in it, I cannot do so in the communicative field of confidence and expectation. For the moment, at least, I must enter the company of the betrayed in order to hear the message. Only after that will I find myself in different company, whether through the working out of the aftermath of this text or through another message such as the next one.

8. *"My Lord and my God!"* (John 20:28) How strange (and inaccurate) that Thomas should have passed through the generations tagged as the "doubter" when his main contribution to the unfolding drama is one of skepticism overcome, of relief and recommitment. Thomas invites us into the field of *the revitalized community*. It has been a long struggle, but the metallic taste of betrayal is gone, and the stench of exclusion has vanished. The movement and flow that previously had come either grinding or screeching to a halt have begun again.

9. *"Jesus, remember me when you come in your kingly power"* (Luke 23:42). I suspect the reason this plea from the thief crucified with Jesus is seldom the basis for sermons lies in the kind of communicative field it establishes: a posture of utter hopelessness for this world, coupled with at best a tentative hope for the

future. The community created thereby might be called eschatological, which would be accurate enough, but that somehow seems not quite to get the point. The unidentified criminal is a member of *the desperate community*. Permit at least a line of speculation here: is it possible we have become so (properly) intolerant of "otherworldliness" and so (justly) annoyed with "pie in the sky" irresponsibility for the care of the earth that we do not easily permit "faith" to exist purely on the basis of what may come after the curtain has finally and irretrievably fallen on our present world? Whatever the answer, it seems clear from texts such as these that membership in a community of despair can also be, at least in the biblical world, a posture of eschatological faith.

10. *"I know who you are, the Holy One of God" (Luke 4:34)*. The peculiar thing about this taunting testimony of the Gadarene demoniac is that it is uttered *before* any healing takes place. Sometimes we overlook that, or at least sound as though we had. It is the posture of recognition in the midst of illness, the combination producing a genuine ambivalence about healing. While this particular text is dramatic, no counselor would find the situation unusual: no matter how severe the "illness" or dysfunction or personal trouble we are helping someone with, there is some part of that person that does not want to let it go. The therapeutic term for that is "resistance," and perhaps it is appropriate to say that in this communicative field we find *the resistant community*. Notice, though, that in such a field a genuine struggle is going on between faith's recognition of Jesus' lordship and the "demon's" tenacious clinging to the status quo. It is *not* the same thing as cold denial or turning one's back on any opportunity for healing.

Here we have ten different texts, then, each making what on theological grounds I believe we would have to say is the same basic affirmation. Or, to put it differently, the "proclamation," in an informational sense, is the same in each. The outcomes for those who receive the messages, however, are very different, because each message has placed its hearers in a different field of understanding and self-perception. Illustrating how that works has been the main point, but there is a strong secondary one: the natures of the different fields (or communities, as I have been calling them in this section) carry major pastoral implications for how people will see themselves and act accordingly. To preach responsibly and restoratively we need to be in touch with those differences, lest our intentions go in one direction while our results take quite another.

Doing that, in turn, requires that we preachers take some personal inventory: What field is most comfortable for *us?* What sort of communicative interaction sustains and, on the other hand, threatens us? What community or public do we find it most congenial being in? The question is, then, who *we* are or want ourselves to be as communicators, and that leads us to the next chapter.

6. The Preacher in Preaching: Using the Self as Communicative Tool

Let me describe a curious phenomenon I notice with regularity in some of my seminary preaching courses and in continuing education workshops with experienced ministers. Often I will ask participants to write an analysis of one of their own sermons, with an emphasis on saying what they wanted to accomplish in it and how they evaluate what they did and did not do to reach their objectives. One might expect (or at least I did) that the sermons would be competent and at times even quite involving but that the analyses would run toward academic dryness—useful, perhaps, but not thirst-quenching. Here, though, is the curiosity: *almost invariably the later statements are more personal, more directly to the point, and more engaging than the sermons themselves.* In fact, they are typically better sermons than the sermons.

Why? The only explanation I can find that makes any sense, and which the preachers themselves confirm, is this: when they are given permission to step outside the confines of what is "expected" in a sermon and talk directly about *what they themselves wanted to do and why,* they achieve a freedom of communication they did not have before. They are somehow able then to use their own investments, self-perceptions, and personal goals in a way that was barred by the sermon. For whatever reason, when they are in the more relaxed atmosphere of the "green room," so to speak, after the performance, they are free to use themselves in describing what it was they wanted to do in preaching. They speak more freely; they are less bound up with homiletical conventions and circumlocutions; they are more "present." And they are almost always surprised to see that the results are better preaching than what they had so carefully prepared for the pulpit.

I believe there is more than just an interesting object lesson in that. Perhaps the landmark announcement by Phillips Brooks in 1890 that preaching was essentially "truth through personality"[1] was premature then, or perhaps in the wake of the neo-orthodox theological excursion through American protestantism in the 1940s and 1950s we grew afraid of the presence of the preacher in preaching for fear it would compromise the wholly other transcendent presence of God. Or maybe it was just that homiletics professors are sufficiently intimidating to have drummed out of their students any idea that they themselves might be an integral part of the preaching event. Who knows?

It is interesting, though, and a little sad, that what you might even call a "movement" toward the responsible use of the preacher himself or herself in preaching, represented first by Brooks and later by H. H. Farmer, John Oman, Harry Emerson Fosdick, to a degree, and Reuel Howe never quite took root in homiletics.[2] The pastoral care and counseling interests did adopt that perspective, but homiletics went off in another direction. A good many of us, for instance, were no doubt taught that use of the first person pronoun was a risky business in a sermon and that whatever truth was to be had from the pulpit would come from a faithful exegesis of the text, with a careful deemphasis of the preacher's own agendas. There was even a strong tendency in homiletics to say that insofar as it was possible the preacher should set himself or herself aside in the preaching event so that either the commanding message of the text or the immediacy of the God–person encounter could hold center stage.

Nothing is wrong, intrinsically, with any of that. The problem is that instead of wrestling with a built-in dialectic of what it means to climb into the pulpit every week, we tried to create fail-safe formulas for removing any vestige of personal struggle from the preacher's work. Let us not beat about the bush: what we are dealing with is a preacher's vocational tension between what you could call *depersonalization,* on the one hand, and *narcissism,* on the other. Somewhere in the middle is the appropriate, even necessary, use of the self in preaching that yields what Brooks in his nineteenth-century way perceived as the importance of "truth through personality."

By depersonalization I simply mean the attempt to remove the person of the preacher from the sermon, both stylistically (by avoiding personal references, for instance) and, more disastrously, in the sermon's inner strategy and structure. Here is preaching that mistakes a concern for "objective truth" for the elimination of the preacher's personal participation in the meaningfulness of what is being said. The question of what I as preacher happen to be dealing with in my life process as I prepare this week's sermon is not allowed to enter the picture for fear it will distort the objective exegesis of a biblical text I aim for, or even for fear it will render me less sensitive to the pastoral issues of my congregation. It does not surprise us when preaching turned out of this mold is often highly rational and intellectualized (even though the actual language used may seem highly charged, as in stereotypical fire-and-brimstone sermons).

The tragedy of depersonalization is that it loses two of the very things it was trying to achieve: truthfulness and pastoral relevance. We now realize, on hermeneutical grounds, that the meaningful truthfulness of biblical texts depends on an encounter and interaction with a reader's own questions, needs, and agendas. Trying to set aside the personal dimension is just as distorting of the truth as is ignoring the facts of matters for the sake of subjective feeling. Then, too, an attempt to make contact with congregational needs by setting our own aside dulls the cutting edge of the best pastoral instrument we have for preaching or anything else: our own journeys through life's wilderness and how they give us both understanding of and empathy for the similar experiences of those who are in our care.

Narcissism, the other pole, is perhaps more familiar and certainly more frequently condemned. It seems to be less intentional than depersonalization: while many of us may deliberately set out to remove ourselves from a sermon, few of us will self-consciously aim to hog the spotlight. Here, though, is preaching that again and again seems to use the preacher's own experience (or that of his or her own family) for illustrative material, or that conveys the indirect message "If only people would be like me, everything would be just fine," or that acts out the preacher's own feeling about something in disguised form, leaving everyone feeling properly guilty and thoroughly confused. The dominant message of narcissistic preaching is often something like "Please like me" or perhaps "When you resemble me more closely, then I will be your pastor."

I have no doubt that much of our fear of "subjectivism" in the pulpit comes from one too many encounters with this kind of inappropriate use of the self in preaching. The demagogues and pulpit dandies are easy enough to spot—and avoid. Less easily reckoned with are otherwise well-meaning preachers who are simply overly locked up in their own concerns without always realizing it. I do believe it is time in homiletics, however, to make a sharp distinction between the bona fide question of the relationship between objective truth and personal appropriation, on the one hand, and a negative reaction to personal parading, on the other.

My main message in this chapter, then, is simply this: the preaching that is most faithful to the gospel, most life-giving, and most vital to its hearers is forged on the anvil of the preacher's own self-investment and self-utilization in the preaching process. It is a question of the *appropriate* use of the self in preaching. As we have just seen in a broad-brush treatment, there are unquestionably *in*appropriate uses of the self that we need to guard against. Our concern now is to sort them out. Let us talk about three distinct phases of pastoral preaching, each with its distinctive self issue: (1) choosing a text and sermon focus, (2) conceiving a pastoral strategy for the sermon, and (3) preparing and preaching the result.

I. CHOOSING A TEXT AND FOCUS

I am not the greatest champion of the lectionary in selecting preaching texts, because I believe it tends to let us too easily off the hook of an important theological decision: determining which text or theme is most needed for this congregation at this time, as well as being something I myself am capable of addressing. Whether one uses a lectionary or selects sermon texts independently, however, there is still a dominant self issue at work. I would call it the question of *self-assessment* versus *self-justification*. We want to aim for the former and avoid the latter.

By self-assessment I mean the process of identifying and weighing the various life issues with which the preacher is currently dealing, on two assumptions: (1) that those issues *cannot help* but influence the way I perceive and handle both a text and a sermon, and (2) that some aspect of my personal drama *may* be able to serve as a point of entry into the meaning of the sermon and a point of contact with my hearers. Only when we are able to conduct such an assessment will we be free to set aside other personal matters when that is best. By contrast, what we are engrossed with *but do not know we are engrossed with* almost inevitably holds us captive and influences what we say and do.

That is a very different thing from using preaching to grind away on our own axes, perhaps in frustration or neediness or obsession—what I would call self-justification. Sometimes the only clue that that is happening is a vague uneasiness we feel about what we plan to say. It may be important to pay attention to that. If I have much of the feeling that I need in some way to apologize for what I am doing with a sermon, the chances are good it is off base. Let us keep in mind that we are talking about *using* the self in service to the needs and objectives of pastoral preaching, a very different matter from getting our own needs met through the process.

It is sometimes a difficult distinction to make, as beginning therapists typically find when they are given substantially the same advice. Donald Spence, a psychoanalyst who writes about the hermeneutical process, speaks of the importance of a therapist's understanding the marginal "gloss" of his or her therapeutic work.[3] By that he means those subtle messages and influences born of our personal issues that affect the counseling process but are often hidden from our recollection of what we have done, or even from a verbatim transcript of it.

Often enough, for instance, I find myself holding back a comment or interpretation in a therapeutic session because it seems to be coming more from my own unexpressed needs than from my client's; at other times I will freely make an equally self-referring remark because the client's issue is the core of it. Sorting out one from the other is part of the hard work of pastoral communication, as it certainly is in therapy and should be in preaching. Getting in touch with one's "gloss" is precisely what I am hoping for for the preacher.

One good way to do that, by the way, is to maintain a "pastoral log book," a journal or diary in which to keep track not only of ideas we have and events we encounter *but also of the kind of investment and feeling we find ourselves having in them.* A good many preachers carry around notebooks for jotting down potential sermon ideas or illustrations; what I am talking about takes a step beyond that into the self-assessment domain: not only what idea just hit me but what it means to me and how I feel about it and perhaps where it came from just now.

Here are two samples from my own log. The five-year-old only child of a couple in my congregation had just drowned, and as I was driving home from visiting them that evening I reflected on how hard it had hit me. The couple was having to cope not only with the tragic loss but also with the well-meant but painful reassurances of some of their relatives that the child was now "in the arms of Jesus" and a variety of other things expressed in the kind of imagery that, given who they were, was only making things worse for the bereaved parents. It had all gotten to me, too. Suddenly a line attributed to Paul Tillich came to me. Someone is said to have asked him what happens when you die, and he is supposed to have replied, "You're dead, dead, dead." To my surprise, remembering that gave great comfort. The very *finality* of death was reassuring, far more so than the alternative picture of the little child wandering around somewhere in heaven. Only then could the stage be cleared for whatever else we wanted to say about resurrection. It was an odd consolation, alone at night on a dark road, but it was real. Then came what proved later to be a key element in the funeral homily: the story that when Woody Guthrie's little girl died of a genetic disease, his wife asked him, "If we had known beforehand that we could only have her for four years and that our hearts would be breaking now, would we still have wanted her?" and the soft, intense reply was "Yes."

Another entry also involves a child (as many of mine do). I was performing a small, private wedding, a second marriage for both parties. The bride's little daughter, about seven years old, I suppose, stood up with us holding some flowers, and as her nervousness increased she moved away from her mother and over to hold my hand. It was the only one-armed wedding I have ever done, come to think of it. What I noted to myself, though, was how that stood as an image of vulnerability, starting over, and new intimacy in the wake of previous disruption. More than that, it dawned on me that I myself was dealing with some conflicted relationships just then, and that is partly what gave such special poignancy to the moment for me. It was a life issue I needed to be aware of. The key in all this is not only having images and associations but growing aware of why and whence they come.

Sometimes self-assessment will lead to a text or topic we want to use for preaching; perhaps more often, self-assessment will let us map the way we are in fact handling such a focus that was selected on other grounds (the lectionary, for instance). In either case, what we are after is that special presence and vitality that only comes when the preacher is using the self appropriately as a basic tool.

2. CONCEIVING A PASTORAL STRATEGY

The question of conceiving a strategy for preaching tends to get neglected in homiletics, particularly when it comes to pastoral preaching. As a preparatory step it falls midway between formulating an objective for what we want the sermon to accomplish and structuring the message itself. If we think about it at all we most likely do so in very general terms of our overall pastoral style or approach, perhaps linked up with those personal issues that a given sermon is apt to touch. I would like to push the question a bit further, however, because it involves a major issue of using the self in preaching—a matter of what I would call *self-enactment*. That has sometimes been spoken of as "incarnational preaching," meaning, of course, that just as God was incarnate in Jesus Christ, so, by analogy, the word of God is "incarnate" in the humanity of the preacher. Self-enactment has two enemies: *self-absorption* and *self-displacement*.

What I mean by this distinction is roughly the difference between, on the one hand, embodying the message we have to deliver (including, of course, our own limitations and sinfulness) and, on the other hand, either being so engrossed by our own needs that we ourselves in effect become the "message" or attempting to cancel ourselves out so completely that we become information-dispensing mechanisms without visible human identity. "Using oneself" in preaching, so to speak, is a very different matter from either "preaching oneself" or "preaching in the absence of self."

Here we risk some very fuzzy thinking about what self-enactment signifies, and to counteract it I want to propose seven very concrete images for what I mean. The list is not meant to be exhaustive, only suggestive. Each image also carries with it an implied communicative strategy, a way of approaching whatever information we have in mind for the sermon.

1. We are sometimes *trail guides,* whose underlying message is something like "I've been this way before and can help make your own trek easier and more productive." We use our *experience,* whatever it happens to be, and strive to be honest about which trails we in fact do know and which we do not. Notice, of course, that we do not make the trip for our customers; our job is to make their own hiking more rewarding.

2. We can be *expedition leaders,* whose task is to organize and coordinate an exploration even though it may be the first time for us, too. That takes a certain amount of *know-how* and *courage,* not to mention humility, which is the quality of the self at work here. It is not the same as knowing all the answers, and success is not guaranteed. The point is that without the expedition leader, nothing would get underway.

3. The image of the *map reader* comes to mind, calling us to make use of *interpretive skill* in figuring out what the map says, even when someone else is doing the driving. There are times when what I have to offer of myself as a preacher is my ability to interpret scripture, or a difficult contemporary issue, or a complex piece of human behavior. I may not have ready answers, or any personal strength to loan people for what they themselves need to do, or any power to persuade whomever is driving to take one route rather than another. But at least I can read the map and let those who wish to hear know what route seems best, where the detours are, and in which direction we are heading.

4. There are times when the image of our self-enactment is that of what you could call the *fallen hero,* who sends the basic message "I didn't make it either, and here's what I learned in the process." We do not much like to talk about using our *failure* in preaching, but the truth is that any number of potentially helpful pastoral sermons have wound up in the wastebasket instead of the pulpit

because the preacher failed—to find an answer for a perplexing question, to reconcile warring opposites, to reach goals of understanding or self-development, to see obstacles and pitfalls in time to avoid them. What we sometimes miss is the opportunity to help other people by reporting honestly on what we ourselves could not do—but learned something about in the process.

5. The *neighboring gardener* can sometimes be a pain in the neck, but my intention here is more positive. This is the friend who says, "Here's my compost recipe, how about yours?" or something equivalent. All of us, I think, lead very hypothetical lives: we operate day in and day out on the basis of certain *hypotheses for living,* some of which work and some of which prove disastrous. If we are growing, we are constantly testing out those hypotheses, adding new ones, looking around for variations to try. The pastoral preacher can use that experience in preaching (provided, of course, that we do not become insufferably convinced that one and only one compost recipe has any merit, and provided, too, that we ourselves have actually tried it, for better or worse, with some results to report).

6. The image of the *fellow strap hanger* on the bus or subway suggests urban frenzy and isolation but also somewhere in the midst of it the cautious message "Do you suppose it's all right if we talk?" I am thinking now of preachers' using their *hesitancy* and *shyness,* their very reluctance to take a chance on engaging other human beings. And let us face the uncomfortable fact that one reason (vocationally speaking) many of us like to preach is that we are sometimes uncomfortable with other, more direct forms of interaction. I am simply asking us to use that quality of the self, if it is there, rather than apologize for it or slather it over with false bravado.

7. Finally, there is the image of the *hostage* whose message is basically "I can't get out of this mess, but maybe you can." Using our own *conflictedness* is admittedly hard; we would far rather wait until we are released and have a glorious outcome to report. Sometimes life will not wait for that, though, and identifying and using conflict that continues to bind us is a self-

enacting strength with value of its own. We would do well to remember that, as Charlie Brown once said, "knowing who your trouble is with" is far better than the shapeless dread of confusion and beleaguerment. That is, when life doesn't seem to make any sense and we are enveloped by a fog of painful confusion and uncertainty, discovering that we are locked in an identifiable conflict that has intelligibility and structure comes as a great relief.

3. PREPARING AND PREACHING THE SERMON

The choice we face in sermon preparation and preaching is between *self-disclosure* and *self-display*. I have chosen those words with a careful intent. *Display* here has a negative, pejorative quality, which is exactly what I mean. It suggests a basically static exhibition of something rather than a working involvement with it. Display is what you find when you walk into a fine jewelry shop whose wares you cannot afford. *Disclosure,* by contrast, is distinctly a hands-on approach, with genuine interaction and shared influence. When I disclose myself, I am making myself *available* to others, risking a certain vulnerability in order to reach a purpose that has fundamentally to do with their well-being. There are no glass cases protecting me from their curiosity—or their sticky fingers. Self-disclosure occurs first to myself when I gain access to those issues, assumptions, and needs that are willy-nilly controlling the way I think—when I "construct reality," as Watzlawick and others put it.[4] It occurs to others when I let them know not only what I am experiencing but also why, as best I can tell, I am responding the way I am.

It is important to say very strongly that the use of the self in self-disclosure need not mean the production of autobiographical details. Sometimes, of course, a preacher will quite appropriately talk about his or her own experiences. But that is not all—or, for that matter, even mainly—what self-disclosure means. Perhaps we could put it this way: sometimes autobiographical detail is a useful *vehicle* for disclosure, but the two are never identical. I think in that connection of three popular and moving autobiographical books that have appeared in recent months: Frederick Buechner's two volumes entitled *The Sacred Journey* and *Now and Then* and Russell Baker's Pulitzer prize–winning *Growing Up*.[5] All are self-disclosures without any trace of narcissism or any stinting on self-criticism. They are not, however, what you would call autobiographies, at least in the classical sense. You have the sense that these authors are using themselves for some other purpose, perhaps to tell people that in a fragmented and topsy-turvy world the details of *their* lives have meaning, even transcendent meaning, if they will only pay respectful attention to them.

One of the best descriptions of such a use of the self comes from an old book by Carl Rogers in which he describes ten key characteristics of the helper in a helping relationship.[6] I have adapted and renamed them to show more clearly how I believe they also describe those properties of the self that make pastoral preaching work. (Keep in mind that we are not now talking about Rogerian counseling strategy, with which one may or may not agree.) Naturally, none of us perfectly embodies all of them, but from time to time at least some of these characteristics come through in our work. You will see, I think, that while using oneself along these lines means significant self-disclosure, there is not a trace of display in the picture.

1. "Can I *be* in some way which will be perceived by others as trustworthy, dependable, consistent?"[7] Here is the quality of *trustworthiness,* seen not so much in any particular thing one does (though of course it will or will not be reflected in our actions) but rather as an inner quality of congruence and dependability. When I begin to hear a preacher, do I as a listener have a sense that no matter what he or she says—or how technically skillful or inept it may be—my life concerns are in good hands? Can I believe that prior confidence will not be betrayed by a sudden change of character? Are the values and style and posture of the preacher consistent from week to week, even when (perchance) my own life seems middling well out of control?

2. "Can I be expressive enough that what I am will be communicated unambiguously?"[8] The word *expressiveness* is as good as any for this characteristic. It certainly does not mean flamboyance, or even gregariousness, either in or out of the pulpit, but rather that sense of "forthcomingness" which lets listeners know that they are experiencing the real person, with a minimum of hidden agendas and carefully camouflaged personal traits. It is the very opposite, for instance, of that feeling you get with some people that you never quite know "where they are" because what really goes on inside them somehow never gets out into the open.

3. "Can I let myself experience positive attitudes toward these people—warmth, caring, etc.?"[9] This is the *warm regard* that became famous in the pastoral counseling movement as one of the essential marks of the adequate helper. It is not always easy to manage, especially with people who seem to defy being likeable or who seem hell-bent on making life as miserable as possible for anyone with enough temerity to mount the pulpit and talk to them about what he or she thinks is important. But this warm regard is not the same as "liking" or "loving" people; it is more a matter of being able to set one's own needs aside long enough to get free from combativeness and so to find oneself oriented toward those people in a demonstrably positive way, whatever the overt level of enthusiasm.

4. "Can I be strong enough as a person to be separate from others?"[10] In therapeutic language this is the question of one's personal *boundaries*. The person with adequately developed inner boundaries does not have to lean on other people for his or her basic existence, *no matter how much sharing of burdens and appropriate mutual interdependence goes on*. It is the difference between the person who holds together independently of others and the person who, one feels, would almost cease to exist as an entity without a "host" in someone else. God forbid that in preaching we should revert to an earlier time when the preacher was an authoritarian know-it-all in an elevated pulpit twenty steps above contradiction—or human interaction. But we have not always successfully avoided an equal and opposite danger,

that of the preacher's becoming just "one of the boys," or girls, and losing that quality of boundedness which allows enough separate existence and distance for us to be helpful to other people. In short, joining other people is different from merging with them, and the difference is a question of intact personal boundaries.

5. "Am I secure enough in myself to permit other people *their* separateness?"[11] Can I, in other words, maintain a sense of *otherness* that allows people to move away from me, not always to need me, even to be negative toward me? This is the mirror image of the quality of boundedness: not only can I stand on my own, but can I allow other people to do so as well? That can be a troublesome issue. Seward Hiltner once remarked that in counseling the two hardest things for ministers to do were to get engaged with people in counseling *and then to let them go when the time came*. Preachers who unwittingly cultivate the dependency of their people are a negative case in point on the homiletical side.

6. "Can I let myself enter fully the world of these people's feelings and meanings and see them as they do?"[12] Here is the overused word *empathy*, which does not mean either having identical experience or feeling warmly sympathetic but suggests something more like a sharing of perspective, an entering into common cause. I do not have either to like or to agree with what another person sees or feels, but if I am to help that person, or be a useful pastoral communicator, I have to be able to some degree to adopt it as a working hypothesis of my own. That is empathy.

7. "Can I receive these people as they are and communicate that attitude?"[13] *Acceptance* is what we are talking about here, though we ought to remind ourselves, as Shirley Guthrie did, that while God accepts us as we are, he does not leave us there.[14] Neither should the pastor. It is a tricky business, to be sure, to be able *both* to accept people for what and where they are and, at the same time, to commit oneself to their change and growth. What we have to watch out for is the subtle but corrosive

attitude of Pygmalion, the idea that what passes for my acceptance is not really that at all in any genuine, congruent sense but is more like a conditional approval against the day they will become different—floating a loan of emotional venture capital, maybe, against a yet-to-be result.

8. "Can I act sensitively enough so as not to be perceived as a threat?"[15] Let us call this the quality of *sensitivity,* or perhaps *benevolence.* It is like what Hiltner has written movingly about as the clown role of the minister, after the humanizing circus character who tames for us the impossible virtuosity of the other performers, lest we feel totally eclipsed in our humanity by what we, sitting in the bleachers, clearly cannot do.[16] When I listen to a preacher I want to know whether he or she conveys a sense of basic good will, of an awareness of my own fragility, and of an ability to trim the sails of his or her faster movement, greater competence, and more knowing outlook to allow me, the seasick passenger, to make the voyage without added trauma.

9. "Can I free these people from the threat of external evaluation?"[17] This is the *nonjudgmental* component of the pastor's makeup, and it is often hard to reconcile with that urge toward correction or chastisement that overtakes us all from time to time. Actually, though, the key thing here is the source of evaluation: can we help it grow from within a person's internalized standards and self-critical capacity, or do we foster the sense that someone—God, other people, or the preacher—is out there grading everybody's papers? We preachers are called to represent what Christian faith holds as the right and the good; but even more than that, as pastors we are committed to helping people lodge those standards in their own values and senses of self.

10. "Can I meet other people as persons who are in process of becoming, rather than binding them to their pasts or mine?"[18] *Openness* is what we are talking about here, even when it is threatening in its uncertainty and asks us to relinquish our fascination with the past for its own sake. The importance of

our "becoming"—rather than the state of our achievement and arrival—gets rediscovered as a touchstone of theological and psychological thought every now and then, through existentialism or process theology, or liberationism, but if it is never quite as new as we might like to think, it is always as important as ever. The pastoral preacher *uses* the past, like a good therapist does, as a gateway to the future. Without understanding it we get nowhere, but dwelling exclusively in it leads us to the same place.

Let me be clear that I am not calling preachers to a standard of perfection with these ten lofty virtues. I am saying, however, that when we wonder whatever in the world there is about ourselves that might be useful in pastoral communication, these characteristics, to whatever extent we can muster them, are as good an answer as any I have seen. Even if what I disclose are my flawed and unsuccessful attempts to measure up as I would like, it just may be that I will have extended an invitation to a journey into life that would otherwise have gone unnoticed and unaccepted.

All of this, of course, must have both a context and some specific content. From the perspective of pastoral communication I believe the former has been badly neglected and the latter bedeviled by lack of integration. Those two topics lead us in the next two chapters through the rest of this book.

7. The Context for Restoration: Worship and Pastoral Preaching

The experiential, psychological, and pastoral dimension of worship has been badly neglected in most writing on the subject, and much as I might like to I cannot make up for that here. What I can do, however, is at least alert you to some questions and issues that might not have arisen before in just this way and so perhaps prime your sensitivity and, in turn, your carefulness about that complex communicative ecology we call worship.

All kinds of clever wordplays on the term *worship* have been used to explain its meaning, which is perhaps only natural since the original Greek term *leitourgeia* was itself something of a pun—the "work" of the people taking place on, of all things, the Sabbath day of rest. I risk compounding the linguistic crimes, but the thesis of this chapter is best said as follows: *Worship is the workshop of restoration.* It is the place where pastoral needs and explicit theological interpretation come together in a unique chemistry whose resulting compound is the experience of renewal and restoration. I want to argue, borrowing a conceptual structure from cultural anthropology, that the restorative work of worship goes on through complex *but understandable* dynamics that, as we will see, relate to social or topical "relevance" or contemporaneity rather differently than we have often supposed. In short, I will be arguing that we have been wrongheaded in much of our understanding of and effort to renew the worship experience and so have been swimming fatiguingly upstream. I want to develop that notion in three stages: first, by examining worship as a ritual/emotional experience; second, by assessing the inner structure or movement of worship as a personal, communicative event; and third, by taking a perhaps out-of-the-ordinary look at the familiar elements of the worship service as, in effect, a "pastoral liturgy of restoration."

We have already talked about therapy as a "safe zone," a place and time of sanctuary in which the surroundings are so structured that it is possible for a person to approach subjects and feelings that in the usual hurly-burly of life have to be sealed off for protection. The same is true—or can be—of the worship experience. It is not a "meeting" or a "program" or (ghastly term) a "situation." Worship itself is more like what Fosdick once said prayer was: "hunger and thirst . . . our demand on life, elevated, purified and aware of a Divine Alliance."[1] In short, whatever else we may want to say, we begin by noting that worship is both a *special* and a *vulnerable* experience. It can be the matrix, the ecologically complex nurturing "mother" of restoration, and it deserves to be both understood and respected. Here is where what the psychologist calls "approach/avoidance behavior" is strongest, in the presence of the intimately personal while at the same time the mysteriously holy. We yearn for what it offers, and we also fear it. We sense that the deepest parts of our lives may possibly be touched, and then we sometimes want to beat a hasty retreat into the safety of pragmatic (perhaps trivial) otherness.

I. WORSHIP AS RITUAL/EMOTIONAL EXPERIENCE

Most ministers spend major portions of their professional lives dealing with highly structured ritual behavior they regularly lead but only poorly understand: the Sunday morning worship service.[2] One will look nearly in vain for adequate literature to explore just what it is that *happens,* both theologically and behaviorally, in the worship experience. We have no lack of information on the history, structure, and even renovation of worship; what is missing are seriously thought out perspectives on its personal and social dynamics as a form of ritual-mediated interaction for which momentous theological claims are made.

It should not have come as a surprise to me (though, in fact, it did) to discover that some of precisely that kind of thinking was being done not by a theologian but by a cultural anthropologist, the late Victor Turner. Moreover, Turner on more than one occasion applied himself directly to the task of understanding something of contemporary Christian worship, using the theoretical structure he had devised for approaching symbolic and ritual behavior in primitive societies. His work seems to be somewhat controversial in cultural anthropological circles; it is virtually unknown, though badly needed, in theological ones. What we can do here is, at least, to introduce him to readers who are not aware of the material and to suggest that when we look at the worship experience through the conceptual lens that Turner provides, something of its restorative dynamic comes more sharply into focus. Three questions in particular are dealt with here: (1) understanding the relationship of the worship experience to the workaday world, (2) evaluating the appropriateness of "contemporization" in modern worship, and (3) examining our perennial conflict between the middle-class civility of worship and the biblical address to the poor, the maimed, and the oppressed.

Turner's theoretical structure and his work on worship are difficult to summarize because of their richness. Perhaps a few of the key elements will be sufficient to start what might become for some a continuing exploration and dialogue. His starting point is a distinction between two major modes of human interrelatedness or "society." One mode is the familiar everyday world of organization, hierarchy, more-and-less, differentiation of functions, values, and positions—in short, what we loosely call the social order. Its dominant characteristic is *structure:* it has shape and predictability and, even with all its vicissitudes, regularity. It is where we spend most of our time. Most sociological and anthropological theory has interpreted "social" to mean "social-structural" in this sense. There is another mode of interrelatedness, however, which is characterized by what Turner calls "anti-structure." Here is a "society as an unstructured or rudimentarily structured and relatively

undifferentiated *comitatus,* community, or even communion of
equal individuals."[3] To this other mode of social organization
Turner gives the name "communitas," partly to capture the
sense of a "modality of social relationship," as opposed to the
more geographical or political term *community.* It is, of course,
exactly that emphasis on the modality of interrelatedness that
we are interested in:

> *Communitas* is a fact of everyone's experience, yet it has almost never been
> regarded as a reputable or coherent object of study by social scientists. It is,
> however, central to religion, literature, drama, and art, and its traces may be
> found deeply engraven in law, ethics, kinship, and even economics. It
> becomes visible in tribal rites of passage, in millenarian movements, in
> monasteries, in the counterculture, and on countless informal occasions.[4]

Where is this other, and perhaps less familiar, mode of
relationship, this *communitas,* to be found, and what are the
people like who display it? Briefly, *communitas* arises out of
situations of "liminality," of being "on the margin," a term
borrowed from Arnold van Gennep's concept of *rites de passage.*
The transitional experience of a *rite de passage* is marked by
three phases: separation, margin or *limen* (meaning "threshold" in Latin), and aggregation. A participant in a *rite de
passage,* whether in the formal sense of a manhood ritual or the
informal but equally potent meaning of a life change such as, let
us say, occupational retirement, first is *separated* from the social
structure he or she formally occupied, then experiences a
period of time "on the margin" of more familiar associations,
activities, and social position during which the subject is in
some way transformed and introduced to the new situation he
or she will occupy next. A regathering or "aggregation" back
into the structure of society follows and completes the process.

The comparison we are after with worship does not have
much to do with the manhood ritual per se but rather with this
threefold movement of a *rite de passage.* We have typically talked
about the worship experience in much the same way. It begins
with a "calling out," a separation of believers from their regular
worldly concerns. The time, the place, the "furnishings" of

worship contribute to the separateness (contrary, by the way to the popular notion that one can "worship" anywhere and any time). What happens then, during the marginal, transition period is what could be called "pilgrimage and address," viz., the familiar content of the worship service. Often such rituals as *rites de passage* contain a symbolic journey, perhaps reflected in ritual movements or "stations" during which the participant is in some way imparted essential information and direction. That is no more than to describe the content of the worship service, and the metaphor of journey or pilgrimage or "drama of faith" is often used to describe its symbolic significance. Following worship itself is a reincorporation into the world, talked about in theological terms as a "commissioning" for discipleship, a dismissal from the special time and place of worship to return to everyday concerns, transformed and renewed: "Ite, missa est."

For now, it is the middle phase that interests us, the "liminal" period when one is neither here nor there, so to speak, in terms of social structure. On the analogy of a *rite de passage* this is what most think of as "the worship experience." One is *marginal;* Turner calls the experience one of *"liminality."* The experience of marginal people, experiencing liminality, is one of *communitas*.

Major liminal situations are occasions on which, so to speak, a society takes cognizance of itself, or rather where, in an interval between their incumbency of specific fixed positions, members of that society may obtain an approximation, however limited, to a global view of man's place in the cosmos and his relations with other classes of visible entities.[5]

The two qualities most characteristic of liminality, Turner argues, are "lowliness and sacredness." The liminal state is characterized by a loss of previous caste, wisdom, and social status but a gain in sacredness and spiritual power. Witness the impoverished, vagrant holy friar or the outcast, foolish healer of mythology and literature. Among liminal people is to be found a social equality and heteronomy that distinguishes *communitas*. Although this is not the place for a full discussion, it may be helpful to reproduce Turner's list of the contrasting properties of liminality, on the one hand, and the social status system, on the other:

Transition/state
Totality/partiality
Homogeneity/heterogeneity
Communitas/structure
Equality/inequality
Anonymity/systems of nomenclature
Absence of property/property
Absence of status/status
Nakedness or uniform/distinctions of clothing
Sexual continence/sexuality
Minimization of sex distinctions/maximization of distinctions
Absence of rank/distinctions of rank
Humility/just pride of position
Disregard for personal appearance/care for appearance
No distinction of wealth/distinctions of wealth
Unselfishness/selfishness
Total obedience/obedience only to superior rank
Sacredness/secularity
Sacred instruction/technical knowledge
Silence/speech
Suspension of kinship rights and obligations/
    kinship rights, obligations
Continuous reference to mystical powers/intermittent reference
Foolishness/sagacity
Simplicity/complexity
Acceptance of pain and suffering/avoidance of pain and suffering
Heteronomy/degree of autonomy[6]

Structure and *communitas* are dialectically related, in the manner of any state/transition interaction. Daily social structure yields to *communitas* experience both in deliberate rituals and in serendipitous events, while *communitas* eventually takes on the trappings of structure, despite frequent attempts to preserve it as a perpetual state, as, for instance, in such disparate but intimately related phenomena as expatriate literary communities, the hippie subculture of the 1960s, monastic movements, and college reunions.

For individuals and groups, social life is a type of dialectical process that involves successive experience of high and low, communitas and structure, homogeneity and differentiation, equality and inequality. . . . In other words, each individual's life experience contains alternating exposure to structure and communitas, and to states and transitions.[7]

There is a dialectic here, for the immediacy of *communitas* gives way to the mediacy of structure, while in *rites de passage,* men are released from structure into communitas only to return to structure revitalized by their experience of communitas. What is certain is that no society can function adequately without this dialectic. Exaggeration of structure may well lead to pathological manifestations of communitas outside or against "the law." Exaggeration of communitas, in certain religious or political movements of the leveling type, may be speedily followed by despotism, overbureaucratization, or other modes of structural rigidification.[8]

Here is the restorative dynamic at work: through an experience of *communitas* a person is changed, by being able, for a brief time, to see himself or herself "from the standpoint of the sacred," as Michael Novak would say, that is, free from the social-structural identification in terms of which we usually perceive ourselves and others.[9] Much the same thing happens in psychotherapy with its "regression in service to the ego" and its "holding" dynamics.

A special characteristic of *communitas* is its power to encode itself in special symbol systems:

Liminality, marginality, and structural inferiority are conditions in which are frequently generated myths, symbols, rituals, philosophical systems, and works of art. These cultural forms provide men with a set of templates or models which are, at one level, periodical reclassifications of reality and man's relationship to society, nature, and culture. But they are more than classifications, since they incite men to action as well as to thought. Each of these productions has a multivocal character, having many meanings, and each is capable of moving people at many psychobiological levels simultaneously.[10]

When Turner wrote about worship explicitly, he took this line of thinking a crucial step further: the symbols created by *communitas* experience tend to have the power to reinvoke that experience. It is as though they in some way "carry" the experience potentially inside themselves, so that early *communitas* is released—or, more properly, reenacted—when the symbols it generated are used once again in certain ways.

Such symbols, visual and auditory, operate culturally as mnemonics or, as communications engineers would no doubt have it, as "storage bins" of information, not about pragmatic techniques, but about cosmologies, values, and cultural axioms, whereby a society's "deep knowledge" is transmitted from one generation to another.[11]

Under favorable circumstances some structural form generated long ago, from a moment of communitas, may be almost miraculously liquified into a living form of communitas again.[12]

The vain task of trying to find out in what precise way certain symbols found in the ritual, poetry, or iconography of a given society "reflect" or "express" its social or political structure can then be abandoned. Symbols may well reflect not structure but anti-structure, and not only "reflect" it but contribute to *creating* it.[13]

That is what accounts for the use of traditional icons, music, or language in *communitas* rituals, for instance, and that is what Turner argued happens in Christian worship.

It is the very archaicness and oddity of these symbols that gives them their power to invoke *communitas*. When Vatican II reformed Roman Catholic worship, Marshall McLuhan (himself a devout Catholic) was said to have been deeply worried that the loss of the Latin Mass and its archaic trappings would destroy the worship experience, a prediction many would argue has come true. The reason for the worry is just this point of Turner's, that tampering with what seem at first blush to be outmoded, incomprehensible, and anachronistic symbols in the name of contemporaneity and understanding runs the risk of draining them of their *communitas*—invoking power.

Inherited [symbolic] forms will not be "dead" forms if they have themselves been the product of "free" religious or esthetic creativeness, in brief, of liminality and *communitas* (between man and God as well as between man and man). Archaic patterns of actions and objects which arose in the past from the free space within liminality can become protective of future free spaces. The archaic is not the obsolete.[14]

Turner's thought is far more complex and far-reaching than this brief summary, but perhaps we have enough of it in hand to illustrate its usefulness in understanding something of the restorative dimension of Christian worship. A major point to be made is methodological: here is a *way* of examining and hypothesizing about ritual process that takes us into the inner nature of the experience itself, going beyond the more external, taxonomical, and historical approach to liturgical study we are more familiar with. Let us turn to the three specific questions posed at the beginning of this section, from the vantage point of Turner's cultural anthropological approach.

First, what is the relationship of the worship experience to the workaday world? It is now common among ministers and theologians to criticize worship when it begins to be "other-worldly" and remote from the pressing concerns of society. Typically, we seek to make worship "relevant," equipping the saints for work and discipleship in the world. Under such banners as "liberation theology," perhaps, we want worship to have a more direct influence on the world of state and structure. The contrary idea of worship as a time of retreat or "sanctuary" is sometimes hard to get a hearing for these days, particularly in the face of the popularity of right-wing "civil religion" and its privatizing, individualizing influence. What we may be missing, however, is Turner's notion that the heart of worship lies in its being a *communitas* experience that is related dialectically and perhaps paradoxically to the world of structure but is distinctly and critically different from it. Worship would be, on these terms, an *antistructural* experience, and efforts to make it "relevant" and directly connected to the structural world would destroy it.

The case could be made, in other words (much as McLuhan tried to do about the vernacularization of the Latin Mass), that precisely what irritates some people about worship—its remoteness from social concern, its ancient language and imagery, and so forth—is what gives it its unique power. A worshiper having experienced *communitas* is to a degree transformed and able to carry the fruits of that transformation back into the world of structure, perchance to work toward its reformation. It would, then, be just as fatal an error to try to make worship a staging ground for social action as it would be to run IBM as a T-group. Unhappily, the religious world has too largely abandoned its *communitas*-protecting function. A lengthy quotation from Turner makes that judgment and poses, indirectly, an invitation to a new understanding of worship.

It would seem that where there is little or no structural provision for liminality, the social need for escape from or abandonment of structural commitments seeks cultural expression in ways that are not explicitly "religious," though they may become heavily "ritualized." Quite often this retreat from social structure may appear to take an individualistic form, as in the case of so many post-renaissance artists, writers, and philosophers. But if one looks closely at their productions, one often sees in them at least a plea for *communitas*. The artist is not really alone, nor does he write, paint, or compose for "posterity," but for living *communitas*. Of course, like the initiand in tribal society, the novelistic hero has to be reinduced into the structural domain, but for the "twice-born" (or "converted") the *sting* of that domain—its ambitions, envies and power struggles—has been removed. He is like Kierkegaard's "knight of faith" who, having confronted the structured and quantitative crowd as "the qualitative individual," now moves from antithesis to synthesis and, though remaining outwardly indistinguishable from others in this order of social structure, is henceforth inwardly free from its despotic authority and an autonomous source of creative behavior. This acceptance or "forgiveness" (to use William Blake's term) of "structure" in a movement of return from a liminal situation is a process that recurs again and again in Western literature. . . . It represents a "secularization" of what seems to have been originally a religious process.[15]

A careful distinction needs to be made, however: antistructure or liminality need not be "conservative" in the popular religious sense (even though it might well be argued that the popularity of conservative, evangelical worship comes from its more effective embodiment of *communitas*). It is neither oppressive nor theologically retrograde to claim worship as an experience of "sanctuary" where people can lay aside their structural rights, obligations, and distinctions and come together in *communitas*. Turner hears Martin Buber as meaning essentially the same thing with his term "community" and quotes him approvingly:

Community is the being no longer side by side (and, one might add, above and below) but *with* one another of a multitude of persons. And this multitude, though it moves towards one goal, yet experiences everywhere a turning to, a dynamic facing of, the others, a flowing from *I* to *Thou*.[16]

Such a perspective would wish that ministers spend less time trying to make their worship services relevant and socially connected and more time taking care that the conditions for *communitas* are met.

Second, what can we now make of the penchant for contemporization in worship? In many ways the point has already been made: if we are trying to create an environment in which restorative *communitas* can occur, purging the archaic symbols of liturgy can be counterproductive. Virtually every modern denominational effort to reform and modernize its liturgy has met with entrenched resistance from worshipers themselves, who typically view each change as a *loss*. Without arguing that change is inappropriate, one can nevertheless ask that we pay closer attention to that resistance for what it sometimes may be saying, viz., that modernization threatens worship with the loss of that special *communitas* quality which is its *raison d'être*.

A new criterion for evaluating liturgical change and innovation might therefore be whether in a given instance it helps or hinders the movement toward *communitas*. Examples come quickly to mind: most worshipers tolerate and even welcome revised translations of the Bible, *except* when it comes to certain familiar and beloved passages such as the Twenty-third Psalm, the Lord's Prayer, or the Beatitudes. Then even the most enthusiastic modernists will dig in their heels, because with those passages we are dealing with symbols that are more centrally associated with *communitas* and are capable of invoking it. A liberal, independent congregation of Unitarian bent dislikes singing many of the old familiar hymns because their lyrics go against the theological grain with militaristic or sexist imagery. But this same congregation insists on keeping the old hymn *tunes* and writing new lyrics for them, again because the music itself is rich with *communitas*.

Even within a worship experience it could be argued that there is alternation between states and transitions, so that in one moment worship is more structural and later it is more liminal. Turner's approach would bid us do a finer-grained analysis of which is which, knowing in advance that transitional, *communitas* portions of worship are going to be the more fragile when it comes to contemporization and change.

Our third question moves in a rather different direction, but Turner's work is equally helpful for it. No one can fail to notice that the biblical address is to the poor, the maimed, and the outcast—emphatically so in the New Testament. The sometimes violent contrast, for example, of a highly paid modern executive listening to Jesus say "Blessed are the poor" has been the stuff of both low humor and real theological concern. How do we deal with the apparent contradiction that in the New Testament the gospel is addressed to the kinds of people who are clearly not most of *us*? How do we cope with the fact that if we find ourselves in the New Testament we will most likely do so as the Pharisees?

Preaching and worship have been rightly criticized at times for emphasizing a personalistic, individualized concern at the expense of people and situations who by almost any standard appear to be far more needy than most of us. In a related way, pastoral preaching has been castigated—sometimes rightly and sometimes ignorantly—for being psychological storytelling and worse, aimed more at making people feel better about themselves than at proclaiming the gospel. This very dilemma of the Bible's intended audience gathers up those issues nicely.

The strain of biblical imagery encompassing the poor, sinners, the ill, widows, servants, children, women, and people of low estate can be read in two ways. In the first place, of course, Jesus *really is* talking to those kinds of people, and no hermeneutical trick will alter the fact. "Poor" is not a metaphor for anything in the texts themselves: poor is poor. There is another completely consistent way of reading that imagery, however: the people it describes are all *marginal* people in terms of the current social structure, just as Jesus himself takes the role of a marginal person much of the time. From this perspective, then, the emphasis is not on the rich variety of sociological labels but rather on the interrelatedness of the imagery: what is being described as the native soil of the gospel is liminality in whatever form it occurs. "Unless you receive the kingdom as a little child," "There is neither Jew nor Greek, slave nor free, male nor female," "He receives sinners and eats with them," "Blessed are you when people curse and revile you" are all affirmations of liminality as the condition for hearing and receiving the gospel.

Now, the point must be made, at the risk of a certain unpopularity, that what the Bible is talking about is not economic, sexual, chronological, or physical in and of itself, and that any one of us is capable of being in a marginal, liminal situation. That, in fact, is precisely what worship viewed in this way seeks to do: put us in touch with our liminality in whatever form it is found and allow us to come together in an experience of *communitas*. That is no license to ignore or gloss over the real and pressing issues of poverty, race, oppression, sexism, or agism. But by the same token, concern for those issues is no license to exclude from *communitas* people who do not happen to be poor, female, old, black, or downtrodden.

That point is no better illustrated than in Turner's vivid description of the ritual "marginalizing" of tribal chieftains and shamans, wherein those who in the world of structure are soon to be on top of the heap are brought low and made sacred in *communitas* precisely that they may be equipped to function in their new states.

Worship can involve us in marginality in two ways. First, if sensitively and intelligently done it can address and draw out those aspects of our real, everyday existence that are, in fact, already liminal—whether it be poverty, illness, loss of a job, divorce, bereavement, dislocation, or anything else. That is preeminently a pastoral dimension, and it is the dominant concern of this book. Second, however, the ritual experience itself can create a liminality in its "here and nowness" so that no matter who or what we were upon entering the sanctuary, we are thrust into *communitas*. Both are exceedingly potent dynamics, and both the opportunity for ministry and the risk of it are high. We will be taking up that aspect of things more explicitly in the next two sections of this chapter.

That is precisely why, however, an analytical resource such as Victor Turner's approach is so appealing and so needed. It offers opportunity for understanding both the uniqueness of Christian worship as the work of the gospel and the connectedness of our experience with all people seeking transcendent truth and freedom in whatever time, place, and fashion.

The great historical religions have, in the course of time, learned how to incorporate enclaves of *communitas* within their institutionalized structures— just as tribal religions do with their *rites de passage*—and to oxygenate, so to speak, the mystical body by making provision for those ardent souls who wish to live in *communitas* and poverty all their lives. Just as in a ritual of any complexity there are phases of separation from and reaggregation to the domain of social structure (phases which themselves contain many structural features, including symbols which reflect or express structural principles) and a liminal phase representing an interim of *communitas* with its own rich and elaborate symbolism, so does a great religion or church contain many organizational and liturgical sectors which overlap with and interpenetrate the secular social structure but maintain in a central position a sanctuary of unqualified *communitas,* of that poverty which is said to be "the poetry of religion" and of which St. Francis, Angelus Silesius, the Sufist poets, Rumi and Al-Ghazali, and the Virasaiva poet Basavanna were melodious troubadours and jongleurs.[17]

Looking at worship in this way makes several key points from the pastoral perspective, and I do not want them to get lost in what is a fascinating subject (the anthropological connection) in its own right. First, the dynamic of worship depends on its essential separateness from the usual structures of daily life. Sometimes we forget this, particularly when the urge to bring about a direct interaction between Christian faith and daily life is strong on otherwise sound theological grounds. We want to see the gospel "lived out" in society, in personal relationships, in the working world; but in our zeal for that *goal* we may sometimes try to undo the very "separateness" that is essential for worship to take place at all. We try, in other words, to achieve reincorporation right from the start, violating the ritual process along the way.

Second, the "address" of worship is not primarily in service to imparting information but rather to facilitating personal transformation. To be sure, the worshiper is told things, instructed, spoken to, led through a carefully designed series of linguistic events. The purpose they serve, however, is rather different even from the same content in a nonliturgical setting. Here the ritual emphasis is on a process of personal shaping and formation that will allow the worshiper to reenter the world of social structure capable of relating to it and having an impact on it in different ways than would have been possible without the worship experience. Let me make a crucial distinction here: I am not trying to "psychologize" either worship as a theological event or the content of preaching. "Psychologizing" is not the same thing as emphasizing personal address and process.

Third, given the complex and delicate emotional ecology of such a ritual as worship, it should be clear that the overall effectiveness of the worship experience depends profoundly on the care with which its constituent parts are handled. I intend here a frank admonition to ministers to be more careful than they sometimes are with the components of the worship service—everything from the call to worship to the benediction (and, come to think of it, what comes before and after each of those marker events). In American protestantism we tend to see the sermon as the dominant and controlling worship event and let the other parts tag along as best they can. Sometimes we are downright careless, as in the worship service I attended not long ago that began not with a call to worship but with the choir director taking to the pulpit to announce that we would begin that day by rehearsing one verse of the newly instituted "Hymn of the Month." Ready, now? I found myself thinking mightily of separation dynamics, in particular how I might arrange to separate myself from an experience that had already insulted my spirit more than it was likely to be able to recover from in the next sixty minutes.

Fourth, when worship is understood from the perspective of *communitas,* it becomes an experience of high vulnerability for participants. Both the overt expectations and the inner dynamic of the event ask us to take the risk of that vulnerability, of setting aside the familiar social-structural equipment that holds life together for us. As leaders we need to remind ourselves of that often and learn to respect it highly, giving it the same pastoral sensitivity we would bring to the counseling appointment or the critical hospital visit.

2. THE INNER MOVEMENT OF WORSHIP AS PERSONAL EVENT

We have been talking about worship in dynamic, functional terms, but now let us shift the angle a bit and look at the actual parts of the worship service from the vantage point of ritual process. We can think of worship as a series of three kinds of "pastoral movements" that fit together to create a unique restorative experience: *punctuations, stations,* and *affirmations.* For worship to be restorative, however, we need to be sure that the variety of things that are done in it are consistent with the kinds of movement they at least potentially are.

The first kind I would call punctuations. These marker events serve to give structure and meaning to the ongoing flow of other events; like commas and periods, they punctuate it for meaning. The call to worship, a prayer for illumination prior to reading scripture, the announcement of an offering, certain parts of the language surrounding both baptism and the eucharist, a prayer following the sermon, and the benediction itself are all punctuations. Without them the sentence makes no sense, so to speak, and they need to be carefully executed.

Punctuations are typically mishandled in two ways: by overemphasis or by neglect. Take the call to worship as an example. Here is a short statement that announces the beginning of worship at the same time as it identifies the oddity or momentousness of what we are about to do. But it is a *punctuation,* not a minisermon. I have heard calls to worship that droned on seemingly forever, with scriptural quotations, free invention from the liturgist, and scraps of responsive litany thrown in for good measure. That is an example of overemphasis, which, in effect, tries to make the punctuation into a fundamentally different kind of movement. By neglect I simply mean a failure to realize the importance of the item, so that through inadequate language or execution it gets thrown away. "Good morning," for instance, is most emphatically *not* a call to worship, any more than "See you around" will do for a benediction. A carelessly done punctuation misleads us about what to expect and creates a faint but crucial dissonance in the worship experience. We are uncomfortable; the structural "safety" has been partially breached, and that can be as disastrous in its effects as a therapist making a comparable structural error with a client—starting a session, for instance, with a hearty "Well, I trust you had a good weekend!" when the client is in fact on the razor edge of despair.

The second kind of pastoral movement in worship could be called the station or emphasis. I rather like the station image, not so much for its association with Roman Catholic "stations of the cross" as for its connection with the idea of a pilgrimage or journey—which, as we saw earlier, is very much what happens in the transition period of a *rite de passage*. In this category are the primary substantive elements of the worship service: confession, sermon, creed, sacraments, offerings, assurance of pardon, different prayers, and the like. Each of these stations is announced by a punctuation. It is important to realize that they are linked together. From a communication perspective, we could say that the message of worship is the interlocking of these stations, so that what is communicated in, for instance, a prayer of confession relates to what is said in a sermon, affirmed in a congregational creed, and so on through the entire communicative pilgrimage.

The besetting sin of much liturgical practice, especially in the so-called nonliturgical protestant traditions, is the imperialism of the sermon at the expense of the other stations. Even if we want to say that the sermon is the centerpiece of the garden, any good landscaper knows that whether it "works" depends on equally careful treatment of the other accents—stations in and of themselves even if less extensive in time or prominence. I have heard many a sermon simply exhaust itself, for instance, because it tried to do things the other stations could and should do in complementary ways if only we would let them. Or, to focus on another station, the ubiquitous (and liturgically dubious) "pastoral prayer" is sometimes the only prayer in the liturgy, trying to cover all the bases of confession, thanksgiving, supplication, and intercession in one mighty heave, when as separate prayers in their own rights they might weave a marvelously involving tapestry of meaning.

The third kind of pastoral movement is affirmation, the celebration (often nonverbal) of various other aspects of worship. If we extended the typographical metaphor, I suppose the affirmation would be something like italicization or boldfacing in a sentence. Here is the role of hymns, sung responses (such as the Kyrie Eleison, doxology, or Gloria Patri), anthems, spoken congregational responses, and the like. Unhappily, affirmations are sometimes seen as little more than filler material, or worse, entertainment (though given the quality of far too much liturgical music, that last is often a dubious appellation). My young children went through a brief incredible period in which their response to encountering something joyful in ordinary living (like a good joke or news of a school holiday) was to burst into a round of the Gloria Patri. Aside from driving the old man mad, *that* is what affirmation is about!

These three kinds of movement are intricately related in a complete worship service (which, when you stop to think about it, is an extraordinarily complex ritual event). The point I am wanting to make is that from the persepective of pastoral dynamics, whether a worship experience "works" depends in large measure on how carefully and adequately the movements are executed. They provide, in other words, the structure needed to let us participate in the experience without being swamped by anxiety, resistance, or avoidance. To be sure, we are courting a paradox here: for *communitas* to happen as an "antistructural" experience requires very careful attention to the structure of the ritual that brings it about. Actually, there is a wordplay going on here with "structure," which in Victor Turner's sense refers to those behaviors, attitudes, and symbolic trappings that govern social interrelatedness, a rather more special meaning than the sense used here of careful planning and execution.

The most basic rule for that execution is this: *Generally speaking, each station or emphasis needs to be adequately punctuated and appropriately affirmed before our attention is ready to shift to something else.* Let us fantasize a little experiment to prove the point. First, remove or dislocate the punctuations with respect to their stations. Begin by eliminating the call to worship and starting either with a hymn or a general announcement. Proceed here and there with such ploys as starting prayers without any announcement of prayer, beginning and ending the sermon with neither verbal nor nonverbal warning, and so on through the liturgy. Second, rearrange the affirmations so they do not fit the stations they normally relate to. For example, place the anthem right after the assurance of pardon, or remove the choral amen from the pastoral prayer, or insert a communion hymn just before the distribution of elements. Overall, simply *remove* punctuations and affirmations here and there, particularly the small ones that may not seem essential. This diabolical tinkering must be done tastefully and subtly so that it does not call attention to itself or seem gross. What will happen, of course, is that the meaningfulness of the worship plummets while the level of discomfort in the congregation shoots sky-high, *even though the actual content and general progression of worship, particularly of its stations, remains unchanged.*

I am not, by the way, seriously proposing that you do this. Similar enough experiments have been carried out by social psychologists in other spheres of communicative interaction for us to know very well what will happen: deprived of those building blocks of relatedness, the whole structure collapses and we are left wandering aimlessly, so to speak, with our emotions exposed to the elements.[18] Many years ago, I came close to physically assaulting a seminarian on this score (he is now a dear friend) after a 1960s guitar-filled chapel service. After the benediction, the players, my friend among them, took stations at each exit in order to give each trapped supplicant a final ritual plunk and a sugary farewell. Even though I *liked* these people, the violation of the restorative structure was so extreme as to threaten real retaliation. *Those* are the stakes when we deliberately work at deep personal levels of people's lives.

I am going on at some length on this rather pragmatic point simply because it is so often neglected or abused in the conduct of worship. Since I often trust the perceptions of children far more than my own on matters such as this, I was impressed by the reaction of my own preadolescent sons to a worship experience not long ago. They customarily worship in a small church where, unhappily, the absurd experiment in liturgical massacre I just described does happen all too often. On this occasion, however, I took them to worship in a large metropolitan church whose minister I have known for years as a stickler for careful attention to detail in planning and executing the worship service. Sure enough, the service held together beautifully, with exquisite attention to the punctuations, stations, and affirmations, their placement, timing, and so on. My children were predictably bored with the content and afterwards delivered themselves without hesitation of the usual negative view children have when "taken" to church by grownups. But then, quite spontaneously and with something miraculously close to enthusiasm, they said, "But gee, Dad, the service sure *worked* well, didn't it?" Offhand I cannot think of a better testimony to the potency of precisely what we have been talking about. Restoration sometimes happens in the midst of grumbling, as surely with children in worship as with clients in counseling.

Perhaps a comparison to everyday social living is in order. A couple I worked with was experiencing great uneasiness every evening when the husband came home from work and the dinner hour commenced. The two small children demanded attention (and food), Mother was ready for some adult conversation for a change, Dad needed to make the mental shift from office to home—in short, the family had to "re-form" itself after the day's varied activities and into the bargain everyone had to get fed, "wound down," and finally packed off to bed, just as in every household. In this case, however, chaos reigned, and not because of any particularly noticeable conflict or uproar. Parents were not fighting, the kids behaved normally for their ages, everyone was glad to see each other and eager for interaction. A little exploration revealed (not surprisingly) that what was wrong was simply an absence of punctuation and affirmation. The family tried to eat in the kitchen eating area, because that was convenient for the children and it allowed them to go ahead with their meal while Mom prepared the adult fare and Dad tried to converse. The kitchen table itself was not really a table but more an eating bar, so that everyone sat more or less side by side, diner style. Occasionally the pattern varied under the influence of television, and impromptu TV dinners replaced the breakfast bar. Your imagination can supply the further details! There was simply no telling what the starting and stopping points were of any of the major events that needed to take place—reentry, dinner, adult communication, playing with children, and so forth. The evening was an unpunctuated mush, and there was no place for anyone to affirm what had been happening by saying, in effect, (though sometimes even explicitly), "We did it, and it was good." My advice, at the risk of being a little old-fashioned, was taken and seemed to work. On several days of the week the kids were fed early and a time was reserved for husband and wife to talk, some days the entire family moved out of the kitchen and into the dining room for dinner with candlelight and stereo music, and so on through a variety of seemingly tiny little moves whose net effect was simply to punctuate and affirm the whole business. Nothing much changed, but everything changed.

3. WORSHIP AS A LITURGY OF RESTORATION

Thus far we have been talking more about the *process* than the *content* of worship as restorative experience, and since ministers are often rather more content-oriented, I imagine that may have been a bit frustrating. Now that we have some perspective on what worship *does* as ritual process, however, let us turn to the content itself.

The three movements, while equally vital to worship, are clearly not equal among themselves. It is the stations, the emphases, of worship that carry most of the weight of the experience in terms of content, even though they can be totally canceled by carelessness about punctuations or (perhaps somewhat less so) affirmations. These are not isolated events but rather stopping points along an integrated journey whose completion is what we mean by "worship experience." That narrative cycle has often been described as a drama. From the pastoral perspective I am interested in how the various stations of worship seem to correlate with certain theological categories and also with life events and emotional functions. It is almost as though the drama of worship is at the same time a journey through the entire emotional landscape, touching in the process at least a number of life's primary psychodynamic issues, problems, and personal functions. What intrigues me, in other words, is the way in which the stations of worship themselves, familiar enough to all of us in their usual theological meanings, also constitute a sort of "liturgy of restoration."

More than anything else Paul Pruyser's landmark volume *The Minister as Diagnostician* is responsible for starting this line of thinking. Pruyser's thesis is that "pastoral diagnosis" of people's life issues and problems can be carried out using the theological categories that are our native professional language. Seven such concepts form the framework of his diagnostic structure: awareness of the holy, providence, faith, grace (or gratefulness), repentance, communion, and vocation. For instance, whether a person can believe that he or she is worthy of being helped, whether the person is capable of realistic hope, as opposed to magical wishing, and whether the person is able to trust the pastor to whom he or she has turned for help are all aspects of what we *could* talk about psychologically. Pruyser argues, however, that for believers they are equally well addressed by the theological idea of *providence:* whether I can believe that in the arrangement of the universe there is a divine purpose toward me and for me.[19]

For each cluster of personal issues attached to Pruyser's seven theological categories we could develop a negative and a positive code, so to speak, to describe in shorthand terms how well or poorly a person was faring in each area. Erik Erikson used the same approach when for each of his characteristic developmental conflicts he described a positive "virtue" to be attained if the conflict were successfully waged and a corresponding dysfunction or problem if it were not.[20] Under the category of *providence* just used as an example, the code word for a positive position might be something like *trust,* while the malfunction would be *distrust.*

On that foundation I want to build two additional points in order to understand worship as "liturgy of restoration." First, it seems possible to relate each of Pruyser's categories to a particular station of worship; second, a characteristic interior personal dialogue or message seems to be present in each case. Perhaps the best way to present the overall idea in condensed form is with a chart. The "Worship Station" is the element of the liturgy in question, as previously discussed. The "Theological Issue" is what we might call the point of theological "connectedness" for that particular station, that is, the element of the total theological dialogue that seems dominant or relevant when we are doing that particular thing in worship, irrespective of its precise content. The "Restorative Object" is the positive code for what we hope people will be able to achieve in their personal functioning, while the "Emotional Malfunction" is the corresponding negative code, the "problematic" that the station of worship tends to address. The "Interior Message" is simply a shorthand way of imagining what a hearer is asking inside as the "precondition" for receiving communication, relative to the restorative issue at stake—the implicit question for which the message is in some sense perceived as answer. Table 2, "A Liturgy of Restoration," is what such a schema would look like.

Let me comment briefly on the chart, though I hope it is reasonably self-explanatory. The point is not that the theological issue listed is to be the actual *topic* of every confession, sermon, and so on, but rather that the issue is a theological frame of reference or metaphor for the significance of a particular liturgical station in the total "restorative drama" of worship. So, for instance, confession is seen in the frame of reference of Pruyser's "repentance," which includes such concerns as these: Is the person aware of his or her own role in the problems he or she faces? Does the person show appropriate feelings of remorse, regret, or sorrow? Does the person feel unduly smitten (passive) or angry (revengeful) in the problem, rather than sensing his or her own responsibility? The goal here is for people to be able to face their own culpability and take responsibility for it rather than to escape it all through some form of denial.

Table 2: A LITURGY OF RESTORATION

Worship Station	Theological Issue	Restorative Object	Emotional Malfunction	Inner Message
Confession	Repentance	Responsibleness	Denial	What are my problems?
Pardon	Grace	Other-direction	Narcissism	Does everything center on me?
Sermon	The Holy	Commitment	*Acedia*	What is sacred to me?
Prayers	Providence	Trust	Distrust	Can I trust anyone or anything?
Creed	Faith	Attachment	Alienation	What do I affirm and engage?
Offering	Vocation	Sense of Purpose	Stagnation	Does what I do matter?
Sacraments	Communion	Relationship	Isolation	Am I all alone?

The assurance of pardon is often a liturgical throwaway, I fear, but it is actually the most direct statement typically found in worship of what Pruyser calls "grace": Does a person know how to ask and can he or she ask to be blessed? Does a person wish to be forgiven? Can a person be grateful for getting something undeserved? The pardon might well be made more of, not necessarily in elaborate length but at least in more careful punctuation and affirmation. (Too many assurances of pardon just trickle away into the announcements or whatever comes next rather than being strongly and even dramatically affirmed by, for instance, a spirited verse of praise sung by the congregation.) The object here is a restoration of relationship to and concern for others rather than a retreat into narcissism, since preoccupation with my badness or unforgivability can be as sure a form of narcissism as selfish strutting. We are reminded that everything does not center on ourselves, neither the good nor the bad.

It may seem presumptuous to offer "the holy" as a theological frame of reference for the sermon, but Pruyser's description of what he means by that category seems remarkably attuned to what we are aiming for with preaching: What is held sacred? Does a person know what it is to revere something, to prize something outside himself or herself? If pressed, for what would one be willing to make any sacrifice? Have we ever experienced a feeling of awe or bliss? The key operative idea here is fostering the capacity to lead a life of commitment rather than that state of cautious withdrawal known as *acedia*. One is reminded of a corny but remarkably apt definition of preaching attributed to an anonymous homiletics professor of yesteryear who would rumble in his best Scots burr, "The purpose of preaching is to raise the dead!" That indeed seems to be the focus of restoration in this station of worship.

Prayers of various kinds seem to connect directly with the concept of providence: Does a person trust the place and people to whom he or she has come? Does a person believe he or she is worthy of help or *can* be helped? Does the person hope realistically, rather than wish magically? What does a person believe the divine purpose is toward him or her? The primary variable is trust, which must surely underlie nearly every definition of prayer available despite other wide differences.

The saying of the creed—Apostle's, Nicene, or some other— can quickly become a dessicated part of worship, partly, I suspect, because we typically can find so little *use* for saying we believe the same thing Sunday after Sunday to the point of overkill. Who are we talking to anyway, and how long should it take them to get the message? It is rather like having to say "I love you" ten times a day until it is simply emptied of all its meaning. Recently I began attending a church whose worship service has dispensed with the saying of the creed altogether, rather to the relief of all parties, I gather. The more I worship there, however, the more seriously I sense the lack of this station, because its absence somehow leaves me fractionally alienated from the ongoing tradition of faith in which I stand. It is almost as though we were having to reinvent the whole business each Sunday rather than affirming our connectedness to all the struggle, agony, and hard-won faithfulness of those who went before. Perhaps, though, this way of viewing the creed, from the theological perspective of faith and with the restorative object of increasing our attachment to both the community around us and what we believe, can put some new vigor into things. Does a person have an affirmative, enthusiastic stance toward life, as opposed to a negative, lukewarm one? Is a person really *engaged* with that to which his or her life is committed? Is a person open to challenges and possibilities in life? There is nothing rote or passive about that sense of *engagement,* and it is a shame if our lack of imagination or variety in handling the creed robs worship of this part of its narrative.

The offering has nearly succumbed to economics. By dropping my weekly pledge check into the plate, or, still worse, by waving it past because I *mail* my "offering" to the church monthly, I miss some of the theological richness of what Pruyser calls "vocation": Does a person have a sense of purpose and direction to what he or she does in life? Does a person feel an attachment to divine benevolence rather than the malevolent and demonic? Can a person receive and value a rich range of experience rather than being overcautious, perfectionistic, or retentive? The offering might be, in other words, a chance to express my sense of purpose in God's ecology rather than a stagnant sense of not mattering. Several examples come to mind of shifts in liturgical practice that bring the larger dimension much better into focus. I have noticed that when occasional offerings of not money but *things*—foodstuffs, for instance, or symbols of something one is thankful for—are taken, the meaningfulness of the experience on these pastoral and theological grounds increases perceptibly. One church I know receives a special additional offering for world hunger once each month, with people walking up to the communion table to deposit their gifts during the singing of a hymn. Somehow that *feels* like an offering in a way the earlier plate passing did not. Finally, I once conducted a series of child-oriented family worship services in which for the "offering" I asked each person to write a "coupon" giving someone else in the room whatever they most wished them to have that we could give. I am not proposing that for weekly practice in formal worship, but it does illustrate what it means to offer a sense of my own vocation.

That Pruyser's category of "communion" should be connected to the sacraments will come as no surprise, though I must be clear that I mean to include baptism as well as the eucharist, with much the same theological and psychological force. Does a person feel a part of the rest of humankind and nature? Does a person feel *embedded,* open to the world, in touch, and united, rather than estranged, encapsulated, isolated, or separated? Can a person reach out and express the need to be cared for? The sacraments embody directly the haunting inner question "Am I all alone?" and offer the sustaining answer of a relationship in and with Jesus Christ as the answer.

What are we to do with this neat system? Well, at the risk of being thought facetious, the first thing I suggest is that we study and brood on it for a while, drawing our own conclusions about what it might mean to our liturgical *praxis.* In the process let us think about these implications. First, the *message value* of the worship stations includes, I would argue, some answer—implicit or explicit, conscious or unconscious, articulated or implied—to the personal-developmental questions of the last column. That is, participants in worship bring a pastoral agenda to it willy-nilly, and what we say and do at the various stations is received, filtered, and interpreted by those agendas; that is just how the communication process works. When we are passionately preaching on the catharsis of the iota subscript, it may help to remind ourselves that our hearers are asking, "What is important to me?" (and perhaps wondering whether the iota subscript really is).

Second, worship may function as a liturgy of restoration without employing the language of psychology and psychotherapy. Pruyser's point was that talking about such things as the holy—what one reveres outside oneself, what one will engage with—is automatically talking about a "pastoral" concern regardless of what language system we use. Our task is to interpret the meaning of those concerns to people so that they can understand them, grow from them, and use them as tools to fashion their own meaning in life.

Third, taking the chart seriously will remind us that the goal of worship viewed in this perspective is not knowledge or social action or church building but rather the restoration of wholeness and functioning in its participants and that *the potential for reaching such a goal is built into the nature of the worship elements themselves.* We do not have to force it, or sometimes even talk very much about it, for it to operate, even though there will be times that understanding worship in this way does indeed lead us to build our messages one way rather than another.

Finally, the chart really does no more than paint a picture of what the outcome of restoration would look like, just as the restorer of anything has somewhere in mind a mental image of what he or she is trying to achieve. In worship we are hoping to provide an environment in which people may, over time, engage their and the world's problems responsibly, rather than deny their roles in them (confession); be free to love and serve other people, rather than wrap themselves in narcissistic concerns (pardon); commit themselves actively to what is important to them, rather than wither in the torpor and apathy of *acedia* (sermon); learn to trust God, themselves, and other people, instead of pulling away in fearful distrust (prayer); attach themselves with enthusiasm, rather than withdraw in alienation (creed); live life with a sense of purpose and aim and a healthy recognition of their own contribution to it, rather than stagnate in the pessimism of believing nothing does any good (offering); and enter into those relationships that form the backbone of community, instead of nursing a splendid isolation and retreating into meaninglessness (sacraments). That is what we hope to achieve as pastors; worship is its liturgy.

8. Restoration at Work: Issue Clusters for Pastoral Preaching

It would be foolish for this book to try to discuss in any detail the variety of pastoral issues, topics, and needs that pastoral preaching deals with. Each such issue has its own literature, both secular and theological, and any preacher seeking sources on grief, divorce, terminal illness, depression, aging, adolescent rebellion, or what have you will quickly be overwhelmed by an embarrassment of riches. Typically, however, those literatures do not even mention preaching. The preacher is left to make the necessary connections himself or herself, and part of the purpose of this book has been to offer you some conceptual tools for doing so.

What I would like to do in this chapter is offer a relatively brief demonstration of those tools at work, using several explicit pastoral themes for the purpose. I will present four "issue clusters," about each of which I want to make two kinds of comment: (1) a short statement of what seems to be the heart of the issue when we think about it from the vantage point of pastoral communication, and (2) a suggestion of at least one possible approach to that issue through preaching. The term *cluster* is intended to remind us that these are bundles of concerns, with any one stick in the bundle a separate topic in its own right though they are held together by a common theme. "Separation and Loss," for instance, would include such specific subjects as bereavement, geographical relocation, grief, retirement, divorce, and chronic illness, but it is the shared characteristic of *loss* that pulls them together into an issue *cluster*.

There is nothing exhaustive about this list, though I do think it is fair to say that any preacher who regularly "covers" it is going to touch many of the pastoral needs of his or her people, in one form or another. These, in other words, are the recurring themes I have found underlying many of the more specific issues of the pastoral communication most of us are called on to do. My primary purpose, however, is to do no more than illustrate how some of the concepts talked about in earlier pages come to rest in specific understandings and guidelines for pastoral preaching. The categories are depression, divorce, separation and loss, and conflict and confusion. They are intentionally four very different kinds of issues. Depression is an internal emotional phenomenon, a psychopathology, if you will. Divorce is a specific personal and social experience. Separation and loss is also an external experience in origin, but of a much broader gauge than something like marital breakdown. Conflict and confusion is neither pathology nor disruptive experience but rather a cognitive condition. Each cluster requires us to think and preach with rather different insights and sensitivities.

DEPRESSION

We probably use the word *depression* far too much. I recall a time in my own therapy when I considered myself quite "depressed." My therapist commented one day, however, "Dr. Nichols, you seem to be very sad." Not "depressed," but *sad*. The difference struck home immediately, because while it was undeniable that I was sad, because of a number of deeply perplexing and conflicted events in my life, it was also clear on closer inspection that I was not clinically depressed. It is too bad that the popularization of the term *depression,* from which not even therapists are immune, has scattered and blurred its meaning.

The point is that depression is both a mood phenomenon that often includes the feeling of sadness and a general slowing down and paralyzing of the entire system, whether one "feels blue" or not. There is simply a vast difference between a low mood and an immobilizing depression that leaves a person literally unable to work, sleep, make love, or contemplate the future in any realistic sense.

Two distinctions are commonly made about depression, and any pastor should be at least conversant with them. In the first place, depressions may be either *reactive* or *endogenous,* meaning simply that they may stem from one's reaction to certain situations or events or they may arise from within the person, most likely as a result of brain chemistry which has gone awry. The categories are not watertight, but in actual practice it is important to have a sense of what seems to be the major source of a person's depression. Though it is still a disputed subject, I think the majority of clinicians would say, for instance, that antidepressant medication is not likely to help a reactive, psychodynamic depression but that it may very well be the treatment of choice for an endogenous one. The second distinction is between *transient* and *chronic* depressions. The former occur, last for a while, and go away with or without professional help as circumstances dictate. Chronic depressions, however, are long-lasting and may be associated with either physical or emotional illness, or, conceivably, with genetic predisposition. Again, the categories are not sealed off from each other. The pastor is most likely going to be more concerned with reactive, transient depressions, the commonest pattern and one which I daresay none of us has completely escaped.

One of the best recent books for ministers on depression is *Finding Hope Again* by Roy Fairchild.[1] His discussion of both the manifestations and the causes of depression is one of the most complete I have seen. The former include changes in appetite and eating habits; changes in sleep pattern (particularly early waking or insomnia); low energy; constant tiredness or boredom; feelings of inadequacy and guilt; decreased effectiveness at school, work, or home; impaired ability to concentrate or think clearly; social and familial withdrawal; loss of sexual interest; psychomotor retardation (physical and mental slowing down); irritability; pessimistic attitude; tearfulness; sad facial expression or posture; recurrent thoughts of death or suicide; and loss of interest in activities once found important and pleasurable.[2] Obviously those symptoms can be coming from other causes too, but their presence either alone or especially in combination is grounds for wondering—and testing out as a diagnostic hypothesis—whether the person is depressed.

Understanding the causes of depression can be a complicated business because there are several. Here, though, is where the preacher should begin to get interested, for it is in dealing with causes that preaching has an opportunity to harm or help. *Loss* of all kinds can cause depression. The rule of thumb in assessing the effect of a loss on a person (whether it is loss of a person through death, loss of a job, a friend, a home, a credit card, or whatever) is that *the importance of the loss depends on what it means to the person, not on its "objective" magnitude as observed by someone else.* Sad to say, that relatively simple guideline does not seem to be popularly known. Preachers are as guilty as anyone of saying that only the "big" losses are of interest in looking for the cause of depression. Not so. The question is what *meaning* the lost thing had for a person. My younger son weathered losses of home, friends, and his parents' marriage with hardly a ripple, but he was nearly inconsolable at the death of a wild field mouse he had rescued from the wood pile—because in complex and partly symbolic ways the mouse meant a great deal to him. We have the opportunity in preaching of interpreting and affirming the meaning of loss so that people are free to take it more seriously—and more realistically.

Helplessness is a prime cause of depression, as discussed at length by Martin Seligman in his book of the same title.[3] People who find themselves unable to influence their circumstances or destinies are vulnerable to depression, *no matter whether those circumstances are negative or positive.* (This is one reason, by the way, that just *doing* something, even if it seems inconsequential, sometimes relieves depression: our helplessness is overcome in an activity we clearly control, whether it is running three miles or writing a book.) The theological message we often give (usually on the assumption that it is great good news) that nothing we can do will affect God's love and care for us is a boomerang: it puts us in a helpless position. The interplay between divine initiative and human response does not reduce so easily to such a message, on either theological or psychological grounds. Restorative preaching would seek to interpret how we in fact are called actively to participate in the grace we have received, the traditional interaction—often lost in today's pulpit—between justification and sanctification.

Delayed grieving, sometimes delayed for many years, is a cause of depression, particularly when the culprit is the inadequate expression of feelings of anger and sadness. I realized to my surprise a few years ago that at any given time fifty per cent of the counseling clients I was working with came with a delayed grief reaction as a major component of their problems. We shall be talking about this more fully under the category of separation and loss. For now, the point is that preaching that helps people complete the necessary grieving process in face of loss has a restorative function, but preaching that even inadvertently blocks that grieving (perhaps under the banner of the "joy of resurrection") contributes its share to depression.

Anger turned inward is often held by therapists to be the commonest cause of depression. Instead of being acknowledged as connected to external people, situations, or events, anger is sabotaged, declared taboo, and directed "inside," where it acts not on the object of the feeling but on the angry person himself or herself. Time and again a depression "lifts," often quite suddenly and noticeably, when a person is able to admit to anger that previously had been camouflaged and internalized. The more we can do through preaching to help people understand and deal productively with the anger they experience, the more we will have done to counteract this primary cause of depression.

One cause in this nonexhaustive list that has an even more direct connection with preaching than the previous ones is *exaggerated hopes and aspirations,* coupled with what Fairchild speaks of as "negative internal conversations." When I try to hold myself to an ideal, standard, or expectation that is simply unrealistic and unattainable, I am laying the foundation for my own depression. Common sense and plain observation quickly tell me that I am not making it, and the ideal remains beyond my grasp or competence. I am very much afraid we preachers add fuel to the fire, again inadvertently, when we "call" people to a standard of faith or action that on any realistic grounds is unachievable (particularly taking account of human finitude and sinfulness, which we rather often forget about). I heard a sermon not long ago on Romans 5, that incredible and, at first blush, offensive text in which Paul says such things as "suffering produces endurance, and endurance character," culminating in an exhortation to "rejoice in suffering." Here is an ironic and paradoxical text that invites us to a radical shift of perception of the meaning of suffering, in part as something very different from our instant "feelings" about whatever we may be experiencing. The sermon, however, avoided all subtlety and complexity and treated it in a straightforward, "flat" way, as though matter-of-factly being happy about suffering were the thing the "good" Christian ought to be able to do, and never mind the complications. Short of the few honest-to-God masochists around, any of us is going to find that advice somewhat incredible *as it stands.* It fosters an exaggerated and unreal standard and aspiration: try as I will, I am not ever going to *like* my suffering, and the preacher who calls me to that unreachable standard has also invited me into depression.

A last cause of depression to be included here is *holidays.* So caught up do we get in the joy and festivity—on both secular and theological grounds—of something like Christmas that we lose sight of an important fact of psychological life: holidays are depressing times to many people. The reasons vary and are often complicated. Sometimes a holiday is associated historically with a past loss or upset; sometimes the exuberance of the season only serves to highlight our own sadness or difficulty;

sometimes the common change in time schedule and structure of the holiday also wipes out a needed defense against confusion and threat. Whatever the case may be, preachers would do well to remember some of the symbolism of ancient paintings of the nativity: along with the rapture of the Christchild's birth there are also visual reminders of the coming crucifixion. Christ came not to cheer the world up but to redeem it: there is a profound difference, and for people depressed at holiday times *that* is the real restorative good news we need to hear.

From this quick tour through the issue cluster of depression there are several guidelines we can construct for pastoral preaching, whether one actually preaches on the *subject* of depression or not. Again, this is pump priming, designed to stimulate your own thinking about possible connections between the issue cluster and pulpit work.

First, while getting at the causes of depression is restorative, trying to talk people out of their feelings is always a lost cause, whether we are dealing with depression or anything else. Again and again I hear sermons lapse into "ought" thinking and language when it comes to feelings: the Christian should not, must not, cannot, ought not be experiencing what we quite patently *are* experiencing with no apparent say in the matter. Trying to cajole people or cheer them up in this way is worse than useless, because it lays on them the added burden of an unreachable ambition. The only word that comes as comfort to me when I am depressed is one that assures me of presence, understanding, and, ultimately, acceptance of what I at the moment evidently find unacceptable in my own anger, failure, or helplessness.

Second, we can help people make a distinction between sadness and depression, on both theological and psychological grounds. Seward Hiltner has written that the Christian has every right to be sad much of the time.[4] Who of conscience would not be if they look accurately at the heartbreak of the world? Depression, however, is a very different cognitive and emotional organization. Sadness may engender empathy and action; depression paralyzes. Is not the message of the gospel that, as Paul has it, we are knocked down but not out, saddened but not in despair (2 Cor. 3:7–9)?

Third, we can remind ourselves that a message of hope that does not take account of real anger, sin, and death in the world is false comfort—and worse. I hold that anger in particular is one of our weakest subjects in the church and particularly in the pulpit. We preach angrily far too much; we help people deal constructively with real anger far too little. Hope rises from within despair because of the work of God in defeating the final enemy, not because we were able to talk our way around or out of the real agony of the human experience. Again and again, however, we misconstrue our preaching task to be one of presenting hope as a means of reassuring people. I simply do not believe that a message of hope can function as a message of reassurance, though I have been told often enough from the pulpit that because biblical people had hope I should somehow feel better and get on with the job. No, hope is a gift of God, a hard-won gift at that, which comes only after I have spent my time in the valley of the shadow. Being there with me, helping me understand it and live it, representing the transformation God promises to work in times and ways forever mysterious and unpredictable—that is the restoring word.

Fourth, we can look again at the role of the Christian community, remembering that the community is formed in many ways through preaching itself. The community works to "hold" depressed people in their isolation and their immobility, and pastoral preaching both calls it to that task and interprets its significance. There are times when the only word of consolation available to me is the reminder that I am not alone. Whether I can respond positively to that or not, whether I lift my head in gratitude or bury it more deeply, whether I praise God for his goodness or curse him for his caprice, the sheer fact of being held by the community of faith may be the only news of any kind that matters much for now.

DIVORCE

Until lately I could say that I had never read anything really helpful about marital separation and divorce from a *theological* perspective. The recent publication of Lewis Rambo's *The Divorcing Christian* happily changes the picture.[5] It is a valuable little book, a personal memoir in many ways, that I believe all preachers should read. Even Rambo, however, though he comes close, does not quite bite the bullet on the vexing question of the *sinfulness* of divorce, and that particular is what I want to spend my time with in these few pages.

Two elements of the context of my writing this may be useful to know. One is that I myself have recently joined the category of the formerly married, and though by the grace of God (plus a lot of hard work) my family and I have been spared much of the agony so typical of divorce, I am still much more finely tuned than I have ever been to the subtleties of how we handle this subject, especially from the pulpit. The other contextual element is more mundane: I have just finished evaluating a large number of doctoral examination questions, one of which called for a preaching strategy on divorce. The results, as you will soon see, did little to encourage me.

If there is a standard, enlightened, "mainline" position on divorce among pastors and theologians these days, I think it would run something like this: God intended for marriages to last, but because we are sinful creatures divorce sometimes happens anyway. Rather than condemning divorce or the divorced, however, we should acknowledge that there is forgiveness for the sin of divorce just as there is for other sins and so look pastorally on divorce as the painful, violating experience it is. There are variations, of course, but that seems to me more or less the bottom line of current thinking, at least "pulpit thinking."

I also believe there are at least three disastrously erroneous messages in such a position, which do far more harm than help in the preaching and other talking we do about divorce. The most egregious mistake is the almost casual assumption that *of course divorce is a sin*. We quickly follow that up with an assurance of noncondemning understanding and forgiveness, but to my mind the damage has already been done. On what grounds do we label divorce as sin? What warrants our even placing something as complex as a marital relationship (or its ending) in the particular theological category of sin? Divorce is a complex of *behaviors* and experiences, some of which may very well be sinful. If I am something of a moral traditionalist (and I am), I would quickly say that adultery is a sin, as well as spouse or child beating, stealing the family bank account, lying, failing to pay agreed-on child support, or any of a whole list of things that *may* be part of the divorce picture. But again, they may not be.

The point is that labeling the whole complex of divorce as sin casts too wide a net and violates both common sense (costing us credibility) and pastoral responsibility (costing us helpfulness). Here, for instance, is a wife who has finally ended a stultifying marriage to an immature, unloving, and uncommitted husband who treated her as a sexual object and their children as trinkets of achievement. What does she hear when we say, no matter how "forgivingly," that her divorce is sinful? Or here is a couple who, after years of the most earnest and responsible effort, have acknowledged that they are poisoning each other's growth and fulfillment. With as much mutual good will as they can muster they face the fact that they are hurting each other more and more and have mortgaged emotional energy that might otherwise go outward to other people, their work, or their children. While nine preachers out of ten are assuring them that the church accepts them despite the sin of their divorce, I find myself wondering whether they should not be congratulated on their courageousness and responsibility. By speaking so generally of the sin of divorce we may also dodge the issue of *real* sinfulness and the need for repentance. If the whole business is thus categorized I may lose the opportunity to examine and take responsibility for the particular things in the relationship or my behavior that were in fact sinful. That would compromise both self-confrontation and growth, rather like the person who makes the blanket self-judgment "I'm no damned good" and thus lets himself or herself neatly off the hook of needing to determine precisely how and where repentance or improvement is needed. Or, as a preaching student of mine so beautifully put it, calling divorce a sin may cost us an opportunity of grace.

I am indebted to my friend and colleague Robert E. Buxbaum for a story that illustrates that point beautifully—though in reverse. When he was a chaplain at St. Elizabeth's Hospital in Washington, D.C., one of his responsibilities was ministry to the denizens of the building for the criminally insane. They had all been tried by the courts and found "not guilty by reason of insanity." That gave the patients a lot of touble, which they freely talked about, because they knew perfectly well that they *were* guilty; they had indeed done the deeds for which they were being nonpunished, and the legal distinction was lost on them. Worse than that, by removing their actions from the legal-moral realm, the designation "not guilty by reason of insanity" made it all the more difficult for chaplains and therapists to help them regain some real responsibility for their behavior, knowing as we do that *some* appropriate acknowledgment of "guilt" for misbehavior is essential to the recovery from mental illness.[6] That, in mirror image, is what I am saying is wrong with spreading the theological blanket "sin" over divorce: like declaring those obviously guilty patients "not guilty" it costs us the chance to take real responsibility for *all* the complex parts of divorce, the sinful and the nonsinful alike.

The principle I would propose for pastoral preaching in and around this issue, therefore, is this: Divorce is not a sin, still less a worse sin than some other things; it is a complex of behaviors that have to be categorized for whatever they are, but the sheer status of being no-longer-married is as morally neutral in divorce as it is in widowhood or freely chosen singleness. If *that* is the foundation of our preaching to the divorced, then we can begin to speak a restoring word.

The second thing wrong with our "conventional wisdom" about divorce is the hand-wringing assumption (again from solid pastoral motivation) that it is an excruciatingly painful, shattering experience. Sometimes it is, but sometimes it is not. To be sure, *any* loss experience shakes one's personal equilibrium and in that sense violates the stability of a once-integrated system. Even welcome losses (the departure of a despised supervisor, leaving a hated old house for a carefully chosen new one, or trading in your rusted-out belchfire V-8) have that effect, and, depending on how you define the word, you could call the result "painful." And I would go on to affirm that there are most likely no divorces in which some element of sadness does not enter in. Obviously there is the inescapable unhappiness of admitting that what we once thought would work has not. My point is that we have if anything these days a surfeit of empathetic concern for the pain of divorce but not enough realistic affirmation of the joy divorce also sometimes brings.

Yes, joy. Surely we are not so naive as to forget with *this* subject what we routinely remember about others in the emotional domain, that it is usual to have mixed feelings about nearly everything and that happiness and sadness, love and anger, joy and sorrow are as often partners as they are opponents. One of the best books about divorce ever written is now, unfortunately, out of print. Bernard Steinzor in *When Parents Divorce* wrote movingly (and out of his own experience as well as his psychiatric expertise) of the freedom, relief, new energy, and unexpected happiness that can come when a destructive marriage is finally laid to rest.[7] I honestly do not believe I have ever heard or read a sermon on divorce that tried to place in theological perspective the joy of new beginning that divorce quite commonly is. To be sure, we can go overboard in that direction as well as in its opposite, something like insisting that funerals are "celebrations" of resurrection and really rather cheery affairs. I hope it is clear that that is not what I am talking about. Let me give a small personal illustration. Some months after my own separation a colleague whom I do not know very well clasped my arm one day and asked, in the genuine, caring way that is typical of him, "How's it going?" "Fine," I replied, really meaning it, although guessing his position I spared him the rest that was in my mind—that as a matter of fact I had not felt or worked better in years. "Is there any chance of a reconciliation?" he asked, still with genuine concern and affection. I was moved, and I thanked him sincerely for his concern, but inwardly I found myself laughing, After the years of hard work I put into getting this separation, brother, the *last* thing I want to think about is going back into the battle! That did not mean, you see, that I was or am free of sadness, guilt, worry about my children, concern for my wife, and all the rest. It most certainly did mean, though, that I could thank God for the new energy and freedom pulsing through me as a result of having ended, by mutual agreement, a lethargic and toxic relationship. I realize it may be hard for some pastors to swallow the notion that *anything* good could be said for divorce, save perhaps for the most destructive and abusive situations. Nevertheless, the evidence from people who have experienced separation and divorce seems overwhelmingly to support this second principle for preaching about divorce: Because divorcing situations differ widely in their character and composition, we need to make as much room in our preaching for acknowledging the positive aspects of divorce as we do for mourning the negative ones.

We have now, however, stumbled onto a distinction of major importance between *theological interpretation* and *actual human experience*. It can be argued that people's experience of something as positive and joyful is no warrant for giving it a clean theological bill of health. A ruthless entrepreneur may get the greatest kick out of destroying his business competition by any means he can lay hands on, but that does not mean we are going to praise his nobility. Here, then, is the third part of our usual pastoral thinking about divorce that I believe needs closer inspection: the assumption that because divorce is not what God intended, it is inescapably a theological negative (no matter what one may *feel* about it).

We preachers, especially, have a way of talking rather fast and loose about what "God intends." Often I have the rather distinct impression that what we are talking about is what *we would prefer,* perhaps on the most incontrovertible moral, psychological, or social grounds. On theological grounds, however, any such assertion is complicated, if not dubious— for the simple reason that making a statement about God's intention also makes some assumptions that are usually not at all clear about the nature of revelation and human knowing. Traditionally, of course, we turn to the Bible for evidence (raising yet *another* host of assumptions, this time hermeneutical and exegetical). Even setting aside these methodological issues (as we must in this short space), we can ask the simple question Where is the biblical warrant for saying that terminating marriages is contrary to God's intention?

To put it bluntly, I do not believe it is there. On the whole the Bible is nearly silent on divorce, as well as on marriage, for that matter, and when it does speak on those subjects it tends to do so by way of getting to a more dominant theological point. Here again we make the mistake of talking about "divorce" as though it were a single, well-defined "thing" when, in fact, it is a widely diverse complex of behaviors. *About some of those behaviors* I have no doubt we can make some "God intends" statements, but then to extend those judgments to "divorce" as a total phenomenon defies logic. I am not uncomfortable, for instance, with saying that victimizing other people for our own ends is contrary to God's intention, and there is certainly a lot of victimizing that goes on in both divorces and marriages. It is painful, psychologically destructive, and immoral; but it would be irresponsible to spread our judgment about victimizing over the whole subject of divorce, even though we do so routinely from the pulpit. The same would be true of a long list of items that *may* be involved in a divorce: lying, cruelty, adultery, selfishness, self-deception, and all the rest.

Rather than argue the case, let me be more personal and tell you what I wish some preacher had said to me at my own marital ending: "I cannot tell you what 'God intends' or what 'God thinks' about your divorce, and so I cannot say—as I don't believe God does either—that your separation is wrong or bad. I can, however, tell you this: however we may stand on the question of theodicy, the bottom line is that God suffers when we do, and every pain we endure is etched as well on that transcendent heart. For the ache of your divorce God also aches; and for the rebirth and joy that come from your divorce God also rejoices. Repent for what you need to, and give thanks for the gifts that come even out of your pain and confusion."

A final word is in order here on the topic of reconciliation— not in the technical, marital sense but as a broad theological category. It was in thinking about separation and divorce that I first began to realize how poorly thought through our usual theological talk about reconciliation sometimes is. We tend to assume that it means an end of conflict and differences, and the establishment of agreement and positive relationship. Following from that we picture "reconciliation" in our minds as something like joining hands again, united in newly established commonality. Nothing I can find in the Bible, however, supports such a democratic, romantic picture (the Bible not being a very romantic document at all, when you get right down to it). What I *do* find as central to reconciliation is an end to mutual destructiveness and the beginning of a "new contract" for what I would call other-serving mutuality.[8] From that a simple conclusion follows: *reconciliation may mean a new "joining," but it may also mean a conflict-free agreement to go our separate ways in peace.* It may mean agreeing to disagree; it may mean fighting hard—but justly—for honestly held differences of conviction; it may mean giving up sadistic pleasure in fighting and retiring to separate corners. The essence of the thing is the end to the destructiveness of an old relationship and the recontracting for a new relationship. That, it seems to me, is precisely what may happen when a bad marriage ends and a "good" divorce takes its place. That is what may happen when a divorced parent, free from the energy-draining entanglement of a hopeless marriage, establishes a new relationship with his or her children, even in the midst of pain.

Let me propose, then, something fairly radical for pastoral preaching about divorce—that God's intention is as moot a question for divorce as it is for marriage or singleness itself, and that no divorce is in and of itself either good or bad, right or wrong. The question is what the nature of a particular situation is and how reconciliation, understood as the end of destructiveness and the establishment of positive, other-serving mutuality, can be achieved. When we have tried our level best to accomplish *that,* we will have come as close as we humanly can to what "God intends."

SEPARATION AND LOSS

The topic of separation and loss reminds us that these categories we are discussing are by no means watertight. Separation and loss are involved in virtually all the others, especially depression and divorce. Here, though, I want to touch on the basic phenomena themselves, irrrespective of the particular situations of separation or loss in which they occur. As before, the intent is not to treat the subject thoroughly but rather to produce some guidelines for pastoral preaching.

It may not hurt to labor the obvious and say that any number of occasions besides death involve the dynamics of separation and loss. The general rule is this: *Any occasion that requires us to withdraw the emotional energy and investment of personal attachment is an experience of separation and loss.* Common instances not always recognized for what they are would include the following (out of a much longer list that you can easily think of):

moving to a new house or city; retirement; job change; a child's leaving home; a natural disaster; robbery; a friend's relocation; entering a new developmental phase; marriage; divorce; the death of a pet; decline of a friendship. All such occasions are opportunities for pastoral preaching. It is not usually the loss itself that occupies our attention but rather the emotional response to it, which is universally one of grief, mourning, or bereavement. That is to say, the complex chain of emotional events that begins when we either choose or are forced to withdraw the energy of our investment and attachment to something or someone is called grieving. (I am taking for our purposes the terms *grief, mourning,* and *bereavement* as interchangeable, though in some contexts they are given more specific meanings; for instance, *bereavement* commonly refers only to the death of a person.)

Guideline 1: Grief is the reaction to all separation and loss experience, in varying degrees of intensity and pervasiveness.

As the previous paragraph described, the underlying dynamic is the same for all such occasions, even though in one case it will be mild and passing while in another it will be severe and long-lasting. In some sense most pastors "know" that, yet I still find it slipping away from us in practice. My secretary, for example, is a devoted Episcopalian who is thoroughly caught up in the by now somewhat settled battle of the new Episcopal prayer book. She likes the 1928 version and has even made what to my thinking is nearly the supreme sacrifice of attending 7:30 A.M. worship each Sunday, since that is the only service in her parish in which the old book is used. Now even that is being eliminated. Sadly, the parish itself (as well as the denomination) is tending to treat the prayer book issue on administrative and educational grounds, failing to realize that for many worshipers it is a severe *loss* experience and that their anguished resistance is not obstreperousness or reactionism but rather *grief.*

*Guideline 2: Grief is intrinsic to the
healing process in the face of separation and loss.*

To deny or to stop grief, when it is called for, is to work against healing. I imagine that most readers of this book are free from what once was a more common emotional heresy, the idea that Christians either do not or should not grieve. That idea is not only empirically ridiculous but also pastorally irresponsible. What more concerns me here is the way some vestiges of that heresy remain in disguised form even among more psychologically aware preachers. What we *do* sometimes say, subtly but still potently, is that because of the Christian faith in God's comforting presence in the face of loss and in the resurrection of Jesus Christ, believers either do not or should not grieve in quite the same ways as other people. In effect, we allow grief, but we either put a ceiling on it or insist that it should be a different kind of grief for the Christian. We are tolerant of grief *up to a point,* beyond which the "shoulds" and "oughts" start to creep in: if we really have faith we should not be *so* struck down by grief, or we ought not feel it for so long, or some such idea. Two theological mistakes account for the mischief here. In the first place, we may confuse theological interpretation with experiential reality. It is a statement of theological interpretation to say that Jesus Christ conquered death and that we shall live again, and that idea has great significance for the meaning of life as I lead it, particularly in the face of loss. It provides a way for me to interpret the experience I have, but it is not equatable *to* the experience. It is not a statement that touches—much less governs—the immediate feeling of my experience of loss. For a preacher to tell me, in effect, that a theological idea and my firsthand experience are one and the same is to invite a form of craziness, whose net result in this case is to compromise the healing process grief represents. Empirically speaking, it just does not appear to be the case that the quality or quantity of a person's feelings in response to loss is any different whatever because that person believes in the Christian gospel. It may indeed be that the course of grieving is facilitated by the Christian belief system. We might even go so far as to say that Christians in theory could grieve more fully than other people if their faith tends to banish the fear of acknowledging the full range of their feelings and thus allows them more effective expression. But that is radically different from thinking that faith somehow fore-shortens or interdicts grieving.

The second theological mistake we sometimes make happens to be especially prevalent right now, and it amounts to a romanticization of death. Again and again I hear ministers speak of death as "the final stage of growth," to use Kubler-Ross's catchy but theologically bankrupt phrase.[9] Death is affirmed, even welcomed in some circumstances, as the inauguration of eternal life. At its most absurd we find funeral services in which the language of loss and sadness is strictly forbidden in favor of celebration, thanksgiving, and jubilance over the deceased one's new freedom. What happened, we might wonder, to the unwavering conviction in the Bible that death is the last *enemy,* conquered by Jesus Christ but at horrendous cost? True enough, there are circumstances in which death is a relief (though, as we shall see in a minute, even then the dynamics of separation and loss are not much affected), but it is still an *end,* a violation of the life process. Death is a defeat. That we want to say it is in turn defeated by God's action in Jesus Christ is on the other side of a very full stop. There is something absurd about trying to turn the very word itself, the virtually universal symbol of ultimate negativity, into a positive. The word that lies and mystifies can never restore.

*Guideline 3: Grieving can be postponed or displaced but
never dispensed with for recovery from separation and loss.*

There is something inexorable about the human healing process. Grief cuts its own channel, and if it is denied access in one area of life it will find its way into another, even if it has to become an underground stream to do it. I recall a rather vivid pastoral illustration of how that process works. A parishioner asked me to talk to her mother-in-law, who was suffering from a deep depression and long-protracted grief over the death of her husband more than a year previously. No progress was being made, and my parishioner was quite rightly worried about it. She explained, incidentally, that physical activity (such as getting a job) was difficult for her mother-in-law because she had lost an arm several years ago. After talking a few times to the grieving woman, I made a simple discovery that proved the key to the difficulty. The death of her husband was sad enough (though timely, since he was quite old and infirm), but she seemed to have accommodated herself to that fairly well. What she was struggling unsuccessfully with was long-denied grieving over the loss of her arm. *That* was the source of the emotional blockage, largely because no one had told her, in effect, that having one's arm amputated (particularly as a result of medical malpractice) was appropriately and inevitably good cause for grief. We would do our people a service in preaching if we helped them understand that grieving for a loss is not an emotional option. Sooner or later and in one way or another it happens. And both "later" and "or another" typically mean trouble.

Guideline 4: The purpose of grieving is not to reinstate the status quo from before a separation and loss but rather to empower the transformation of people and situations who will never be the same again.

There is a subtle difference here that sometimes gets blurred. Ministers and laypeople began to take a more active interest in death and loss perhaps twenty years ago when books, seminars, and study courses on the subject started to proliferate. Grieving itself as a psychological phenomenon has strangely enough only been studied systematically during the last generation, beginning in some ways with Eric Lindemann's landmark study of the Coconut Grove fire.[10] An early idea was that the function of grieving was to allow a bereaved person successfully to "disconnect" from the lost person or thing, appropriately reinvest his or her attachment elsewhere in due time, and so be restored emotionally, socially, and intellectually to the *status quo ante mortem,* so to speak. That was an incredibly naive and logically fallacious thing to believe, but most of us did so enthusiastically. When people gave evidence of continuing to show the effects of loss in their lives, we tended to say that somehow the grief process had not been successfully "completed."

Now we realize the untenability of such a position. When a loss occurs, particularly a major one for a person, a permanent change has taken place in that person's history and psychic economy. The plain fact is that we will never be the same again because the world has changed irrevocably: what is gone is gone. We will not always mourn and be sad, but neither will we forget. We have been changed, and the purpose of grieving is to enable that change to occur completely, not to erase the loss from our experience like the high tide removes today's footprints from the beach. I once delivered Arthur John Gossip's famous sermon about the death of his wife, "But When Life Tumbles In, What Then?" and an older woman hearer who had lost her husband and then remarried well many years before quietly wept through the whole thing. Afterwards she said, with a great sense of emotional togetherness and presence, "You never forget, you know. Jim will always be a part of me." She was not grieving, nor was she the victim of an unsuccessful bereavement. She was simply stating the truth and reflecting the joy for her of having been transformed enough by her grief that she could live fully in a situation and as a person who would never be the same as before her husband, one night after dinner, quietly died in her arms.

Guideline 5: About grief as about any other emotion it will not hurt to remind ourselves that it is morally neutral.

Feelings, as we have said previously, are neither right nor wrong; only about *actions* do we make moral judgments. Grief may be appropriate or inappropriate, helpful or unhelpful, realistic or distorted, positive or negative—but not right or wrong. Most preachers these days would not come right out and say that a grieving person's feeling is *wrong;* what worries me is the way we sometimes imply that judgment (even when intellectually we know better) in our attempt to offer people Christian hope.

That sort of thing may be more likely to happen when we come to what I regard as the most difficult of the many ingredients of grief—anger at the lost person or thing. When all about us people are praising the memory of dear Harry and feeling sad at his untimely demise, it may be hard to keep from dubbing as "wrong" his family's anger that Harry abandoned them by dying, anger all the more appropriate when they recall his complicity in the departure by smoking three packs of cigarettes a day and not believing in home mortgage life insurance.

Guideline 6: Stoic fortitude and emotional overcontrol
are signs that a person's reaction to separation and loss is
stymied, not that he or she is "doing beautifully."

Yes, there is something in all of us that admires heroic composure and the capacity to carry on in the face of adversity, but that is not quite the same thing. The young widow in a funeral I once conducted insisted on standing in the narthex after the service to greet her husband's friends. The funeral director doubted she could bring it off and kept urging me to stop her, but I knew her rather better. She stood there, often with tears streaming down her face, and with her shared grief quietly repaid each worshiper the countless gifts of love she and her husband had received during his long illness. She was controlled, yes, but not blocked. Through the visibility of her own grief she was, in effect, allowing the rest of us to express ours. Sometimes, though, when feelings are florid even the most responsible of us longs for a little fortitude and self-containment. Those are precisely the times when we need this guideline, lest both in our personal interaction and in our preaching we subtly reward what frankly makes us more comfortable and forbid what really does the most good.

It must also be emphasized that serious grieving takes a long time. John Bowlby found in his extensive research on separation and loss that a bereaved spouse typically does not complete the grief process for at least a full year, often several years.[11] I used to say to bereaved parishioners that at least one year was necessary if for no other reason than that it literally took that long to get through all the anniversaries, events, and seasons that had been shared. Let us beware inadvertently making a model of Theodore Roosevelt, who after his first wife died, decamped to his western ranch, indulged in a month of frenzied, solitary big-game shooting, and thereafter never spoke her name again for the rest of his life![12]

Guideline 7: The purpose of preaching in separation and loss situations is to help people grieve rather than to take away their pain.

That can be a very difficult choice. Our whole pastoral commitment is to relieving suffering, and I doubt that any pastor has a harder time of it than when having to set aside short-term comfort for the sake of longer-term healing. Perhaps, though, it will be at least a little freeing to keep this principle in mind: Very little we can say from the pulpit will in any appreciable way reduce the pain of loss, which is going to go its own way pretty much despite what we say or do. What we *can* help with, however, is people's understanding of and participation in the loss experience in a Christian perspective, affirming that real resurrection comes only after real death and that God mysteriously works through pain rather than around it. The preaching of a funeral sermon or meditation may very well be the formal beginning of that interpretative process.

Preaching in a loss situation is a seed-sowing operation. Someday parts of what we say may strike root in new understanding and perception. It is not so much that the content of what we say in a given sermon will itself be remembered but rather that we introduce people even in their distraughtness to a different way of seeing things. We begin a restorative, reconstructive process whose outcome will look very different from anything we might picture now at the start of it. The important thing is that it is begun and that we all know it. The *announcement* of good news is not, after all, its complete and final explication. We loan people, as I have said in earlier pages, a "stronger sense of reality," and it is the sense of that happening rather than the remembered content of the words that does the pastoral communicative work. To be sure, the liturgy, the ways we conduct ourselves, the basic pastoral care we offer may all give comfort. Paradoxically, though, they probably do that best when their underlying intent is to help people grieve well rather than to relieve pain.

Guideline 8: Grief is a complex emotional experience,
combining a helter-skelter mixture of feelings, including
sadness, anger, guilt, relief, joy, and anxiety.

Because the popular image of grief stresses sadness, people may sometimes run into difficulty when they find themselves also feeling, let us say, unexpected happiness or ferocious anger. People are quite capable of experiencing at one and the same time sharply irreconcilable feelings—ambivalence, do not forget, is the normal state of emotional affairs much of the time. The mischief creeps in when those same people get the idea that it is somehow inappropriate or "wrong" to have contradictory feelings. Then our task, perhaps quite explicitly in preaching, is to teach them otherwise and to give them permission to use the full range of their emotional capability. I vividly recall the first significant death I experienced, that of my paternal grandfather when I was a boy. He was by all accounts a difficult man who inspired passionate love and devotion among many (his grandson included) but who could also be impatient, demanding, and sharp-tongued. My mother, not long after the death, made a comment which, in my own intense grief, I thought was misplaced at the time but have long since come to be grateful for. She said that while my grandmother was surely sad at my grandfather's death, she must also be somewhat relieved, because beloved though he was he had been a terribly difficult man to live with. Perhaps that was a little confusing to a twelve-year-old boy (though I realize now the truth of it was inescapable even then), but it taught me something vitally important about the complexity of grief feelings. My mother's interpretation was a great gift.

My own experience is that two components of grief give particular trouble to a lot of people: anger at the person (or thing) lost, and the beginning of relief when the intensity of grief starts to ease. In our pastoral communication we would do well to pay special attention to those facets. Even such a simple thing as reminding someone that their anger at a dead loved one cannot hurt the person in the slightest can be a significant opening of perception. Anger is as natural and inevitable in the face of loss as is sadness. The idiom "He died on me" says it all: something in us has been violated by the very person who has died.

Again and again I have seen people slowly coming through their grief catch themselves feeling better one day and then promptly dive back into misery. I have done it myself. Why? Sometimes because feeling better seems a betrayal of what has been lost—almost dishonorable. Sometimes because feeling better thrusts us into more independence and self-reliance just when we have gotten rather comfortable with the attention that seems to come with misery. Sometimes because feeling better makes us confront the warts-and-all reality of who or what we have lost rather than the positive idealization with which we have momentarily comforted ourselves. Whatever the reason, the emergence from grief is as critical a pastoral moment as is plunging to its depths and may call for even more careful interpretation. Why, I wonder, do we have at least a little preaching on sadness and loss but practically none that I am aware of on the vicissitudes of recovery?

Guideline 9: Pay special attention to anniversaries
of separation and loss experiences.

Here is an emotional dynamic, often unconscious, that is

both potent and largely unknown to most people (including a surprising number of mental health professionals). Anniversaries of significant experiences tend to recapitulate the feelings of the original experience, particularly where loss is concerned. They are therefore crucial but largely neglected occasions for pastoral care and for preaching, because it is almost as though we are given a chance to relive and perhaps to relearn the original troublesome experience.

The term *anniversary* is meant literally—the more or less exact date of a past event in yearly increments. A rule of thumb that has served me and others well in counseling is this: When a client suddenly seems agitated or depressed and no apparent precipitating reason can be found in the here-and-now, look for an anniversary. Often merely identifying the anniversary reaction is sufficient to loosen its hold, and people who do not know about such things are almost invariably surprised and then relieved to learn that such things happen (frequently) and are entirely normal, even helpful.

Two brief examples can illustrate the way the process works. I once worked on grief with a couple whose young adult son had committed suicide after a years-long battle with drug abuse and schizophrenia. A year or so later the father came to me informally for a brief followup and wanted to describe what had happened on the anniversary of his son's death, two years after the event. He and his wife had acknowledged to each other that morning before he left for work that it was the day, and the father put it out of mind after that. Later, sitting at his desk in the afternoon, he suddenly felt weak and unaccountably sad and found himself weeping openly. He was frightened, because even though he intellectually "knew" it was the anniversary of his son's death, he did not connect that simple fact with what he was now going through. Suddenly it hit him, as he looked at the clock to discover that his "spell" had begun at precisely the hour the young man's fatal auto accident had occurred.

Here is another example, one that happens to be as fresh as this morning's writing. For the last four days or so I have felt myself more disoriented and less energetic than circumstances warrant. Yesterday, for some unknown reason, things got very much better, and last night I had a vivid and complex dream about a parish I once served. This morning it came to me (not without some amusement, considering my profession and also the simple fact that I was to start writing this morning on the subject of anniversaries!): today was the very anniversary of my arrival at that dreamt-of parish, and the previous four days were a recapitulation of the long cross-country drive, freighted as it had been with many unresolved separation feelings about my previous location and anxieties about my new one.

I would draw three object lessons from that personal vignette. One is the relief that comes from realizing that baffling emotional experiences *do* have explanations and can be interpreted. The net gain is an increase in self-control and self-understanding. The second is, again, how little attention the unconscious pays to the passage of time. The separation event I was reacting to had occurred fourteen years ago! Anniversary reactions do not happen annually, and sometimes it is hard to explain why, all of a sudden, the anniversary gets "celebrated." The third is the importance of being able to stay in touch with our past histories *as histories* that can be celebrated, mourned, or laughed at as the occasion warrants but into which we are not locked as perpetual "presents." The anniversary reaction and its interpretation allowed that, allowed me to take another step toward "completing" the emotional journey from past to present that all of us are always trying to make.

It is probably easier to see implications in anniversaries for individual pastoral care than for preaching, and any pastor would be well advised to keep a careful date record of things that happen to his or her people so that the anniversaries can be heeded. Let us not forget, though, that congregations, too, have loss experiences that generate anniversaries, and they might be important preaching occasions. The departure of previous ministers, the destruction of a previous building, relocation of various members of the congregation (or perhaps of the whole congregation itself), deaths that have affected the people widely, old church conflicts or splits, or community problems and disasters are all common occasions that can be expected to generate some form of anniversary reaction throughout the congregational system. Here, perhaps, is one clear case when Harry Emerson Fosdick's old definition of pastoral preaching rings literally true: it is "pastoral counseling on a group scale."[13]

Guideline 10: Let me bring much of this together into *three objectives for preaching in the separation and loss environment.*

These will not tell you what to say but are intended to provide a theoretical foundation or strategy for what we can aim for as a purpose in this kind of pastoral preaching. To do so I will enlist the help of two major psychiatric writers on separation and loss, John Bowlby[14] and Robert Jay Lifton[15] (whose works are both monumental and irreplaceable in their own rights). Bowlby in his pioneering work with infants who had been separated from their parents observed that a typical separation reaction included three progressively more serious phases. The first is *protest,* the familiar crying and flailing around that children do when parents leave. The second he called *despair,* a more serious though less vocal phenomenon that seems to involve a coming apart of the child's inner coherence, a sad confusion. The third and most dangerous phase of the separation reaction is *detachment,* a quiet resignation in which the infant appears unable to move (emotionally or even physically) and has lost the ability to form relationships even of protest.

Lifton, in his own paradigm, believes that what we mean by life consists of three things and that their absence means death, even in the literal, physical sense. That is, these concepts apply to the total psychobiological being and operate simultaneously at emotional, biological, and social levels. The first is a sense of *connection* and *continuity.* We feel ourselves part of a total world, community, or scene that becomes a life-giving context for us, both emotionally and physically. Its opposite is *separation,* a form of "death" familiar to us in the Bible's palpable metaphor "clean cut off." The second component is *integrity,* the sense of something holding us together and in a literal physical sense, the inter-working of the body's systems. Its opposite is *fragmentation.* When the "integrity" of an airplane frame is violated, it crashes, and when a human being disintegrates, that is one of the signs we have of death. The third requisite for life is *movement.* When all movement in the body stops, *stasis* has taken place and we are dead. Similarly in the psychological domain, the paralyzed inability to "move" in relatedness to objects of the outer world is a form of death; when it crosses that permeable boundary between mind and body, it becomes literal, as, for instance, in voodoo death.[16]

The two conceptual frameworks, Bowlby's and Lifton's, are remarkably parallel and can give us a way of describing objectives for preaching in the face of separation and loss. The first is nurturing what Lifton calls appropriate "death imagery" leading to "the sense of immortality." In Christian terms, that is, we can help people develop through their own imagery the meaning of the hope of resurrection. What that accomplishes, in Lifton's terms, is a restoration of *the sense of connection and continuity*—to other people, to one's own past, to the church, to God. We can seek to overcome separation by fostering a sense of relatedness. Bowlby found in a study of recent widows, for instance, that while Christian ideology did not noticeably help the grieving process, the presence in the mourner of some appropriate imagery of reunion in due time with the deceased did facilitate the course of grief and reconnection to the world.

A second objective is reviving and guiding the search for inner forms of meaningfulness—in short, the restoration of what Lifton calls integrity. Perhaps that is what the biblical metaphor means when it speaks of dying to the old and being alive to the new. What I mean as a human being, in other words, gets determined not by outer events or accomplishments but rather by the constant search for internal coherence.

The "death and rebirth of inner forms," in Lifton's phrase, is the only way we have of warding off despair and disintegration.[17]

A third objective is fostering a sense of self-reliance based on trust in Jesus Christ through the trusted community of others. That, of course, is a dialectic: we do not get self-reliance by cutting ourselves off from others, nor do we get community by relinquishing our own inner integrity. Held in tension, the two give movement, the third of Lifton's components of life. The trust in Jesus Christ both addresses my individual integrity and thrusts me into a community of others. Community is both the seedbed and the fruit of the trust in Jesus; the two can never be bracketed apart, and keeping alive their moving interconnectedness is part of the restorative work of preaching.

CONFLICT AND CONFUSION

A preacher friend of mine once said, "If you haven't preached a bomb in the last six weeks or so, you probably haven't been preaching." Likewise, I would say that if you have not dealt with conflict lately, you probably have not been pastoring. It comes with the territory. Whenever we deal with life-investment issues and dynamics, we are going to encounter conflict—if we are doing anything right. Much has been written on the subject, enough so that these days we hardly have to persuade ministers that conflict is both to be expected as the context we work in and to be welcomed as the opportunity for development and growth. What I have not seen given enough attention, however, is how conflict as a pastoral dynamic can be addressed in preaching, and that is the focus of this closing section.

To begin with, we need a simple working definition of conflict. Here is one (among many) that I like: *the opposition of forces, neither of which can be denied and both of which claim legitimacy.* The cutting edge of that is the equilibrium that conflict represents: both sides have an equal claim. If you can vote the opposition out of existence, on logical or moral or any other grounds, then you may have antagonism or disagreement or antinomy, but you do not have *conflict* in the sense we intend it here.

For example, if I come home in the evening, not having seen my children all day, and I want to give them some attention by playing a game and also to give myself a breather by working in the garden, that is a conflict for me. On the other hand, if I have just spent an hour playing Trivial Pursuit with my sons and I now want to go work in the garden for a while, but they want me to start playing soccer, I have a disagreement but not a conflict in the same sense, because the sides are not equally compelling any more.

As I talk about conflict I am working on the basis of four operating premises. The first is attributed to Sigmund Freud and is expressed in his delightfully expressive metaphor of the "psychic soldiers." Emotional energy is like an army of soldiers, he is supposed to have said. At the point of each unresolved conflict in our lives, the unconscious must leave a garrison of those soldiers behind to keep the still volatile issue under guard lest it erupt. That dynamic has two effects. In the first place, as time goes by and more and more unresolved conflicts accumulate, fewer and fewer soldiers are available for guard duty, and less emotional energy remains for the daily business of living and coping. Then when pressure mounts, the unconscious retreats to a previous outpost where the soldiers are, and unresolved conflict is reawakened, in symbolic form, by contemporary conflicts of the same ilk. We saw that at work with unresolved grief in the previous section. In short, unresolved conflict places a lien on our emotional resources and becomes an order of business that keeps coming up again and again even when it is long out of date in any historical sense.

The second premise is from Karl Barth, whose theology is based on the idea of "crisis," the conflict between human sinfulness and transcendent grace. Ulrich Simon refers to it as "the conflict continuum of the universe."[18] The gap between humanity and God is never bridged from the human side; there remains forever a dichotomy between the two, leading us to say that in this cosmic sense, as well as in more mundane ways, conflictedness is the basic natural state of human beings. It is not a theological emergency, in other words, that has to be gotten rid of for us to be about the business of faith. Quite the contrary, conflict is the precondition of faith.

The third premise owes much to psychological studies of creativity and tells us essentially that conflict is the seedbed of creative growth. All growth—cellular, intellectual, social, emotional—proceeds through the disintegration of an existing equilibrium and then a reintegration at a new level of development, awareness, or functioning. Conflict can be the occasion for such a disintegration/reintegration dynamic, a paradigm case being the creative act itself, proceeding from being locked in conflictedness through a burst of new awareness that resolves the conflict and produces a creative product—whether a concerto, an insight, or the theory of relativity. Conflict is not the enemy of creative growth, then, but something more like its parent.

The fourth premise makes a distinction between *conflict* and *confusion,* positing that sometimes conflict represents a clarifying and healing of confusion. When we are confused, the terms of our difficulty are not clear; the word itself suggests fogginess on the boundaries, as though we did not know what we were about or what our choices were. Some while ago, for instance, I found myself anxious and confused with no idea why. I remebered that in a phone call the previous day my father had mentioned that he soon had to undergo uncomplicated prostate surgery about which neither he nor the doctors were in the slightest worried. Suddenly I realized that I was no longer anxious or confused: I was *conflicted* about whether to travel to be with him in the surgery or stay home for some other pressing responsibilities. The conflict had clarified the confusion.

By now you may well be wondering what kind of conflict I am talking about, and the answer is many kinds, provided they meet the initial definition. There may be relational conflict among people; "political" conflict about positions on various issues; situational conflict surrounding the circumstances we are in (as with the pending surgery); theological conflict between what we believe to be God's will and human initiative; emotional conflict involving opposing desires or claims; organizational conflict having to do with forces of change and consolidation in group life; perceptual conflict between ordinary and extraordinary or religious views of the same objects or situations; historical conflict regarding opposing beliefs, allegiances, or entities; and developmental conflict coming from stages of human growth in which antagonistic forces are arrayed against each other, as, for instance, in the developmental psychology of Erik Erikson.

Almost invariably in a discussion of this sort an objection is quite seriously raised: Is it not irresponsible to inflict conflict on people instead of preaching peace and reconciliation, trying thereby to reduce conflict? The answer is that it might be irresponsible if there were no conflict "out there" to begin with. Here is every therapist's dilemma. When from *our* professional point of view a conflict that needs to be dealt with is curtailing a person's functioning and growth, but the person himself or herself seems unruffled by or unaware of it, do we speak or keep silent? The best answer I can give for preaching, especially biblically based pastoral preaching, is this: the human conflicts and dilemmas one encounters in the Bible and in the tradition of the church are already "ours" in the sense that they are givens in the created order and human situation. Exposing a conflict with which we are already beset, like it or not, is not at all the same thing as inflicting it on people who would otherwise escape unscathed. When we deal responsibly with conflict in preaching we are dealing with something that is already there and that, consciously or unconsciously, our people are already grappling with. What we need to do next is provide some guidelines for that work.

From a communication point of view the similarities in that earlier list of types of conflict outweigh the differences, because all those kinds of conflict are mediated through messages. That means that from the point of view of pastoral preaching we can make some generalizations to guide our more specific sermon work. I would want to say that the overall objective of pastoral preaching regarding conflict involves a half dozen essential elements. With these in view we can be in a position to tap the growth-facilitating power of conflict in such a way that the words of our preaching become restorative.

1. The *identification* of conflict is the starting point. Sometimes the conflictedness with which we wish to deal will be represented in a biblical text, sometimes in personal relationships of the hearers, sometimes within the organizational dynamics of the church. What is needed is a diagnosis of the situation so that its terms are clear.

2. *Energizing* people for participation in the conflict is the essential next step. The alternatives are more depressingly familiar: we may try to smooth it over in a false harmony, to protect ourselves from it in diversion or self-justification, to escape it by moving to other issues, or to deny it altogether. Energizing, by contrast, is a form of permission giving, whereby people are not just allowed but encouraged to engage the conflictual issues before them.

3. *Contextualizing* the conflict in theological perspective means relating it to the ultimate concerns of hearers, to the foundational issues of human existence in light of the gospel. We want to make it clear, in other words, what the theological values and implications may be of issues that might otherwise slide completely into the nontheological realm.

4. *Focusing* the conflict begins to be harder work, because this fourth element means closing off false or premature escapes from it. The preacher may want to say quite explicitly, "It looks like this or that will get us out from under the trouble, but no, here is how it doesn't do the work." This I believe to be the heart of that badly abused concept, "prophetic preaching," and the importance of it is probably worth more than the few lines I am giving it here. The bibilical tradition of prophetic preaching is not condemnation but rather focusing the conflict between

divine plan and human action or commitment. That is very different from clobbering people with imperatives, confrontations, accusations, or, still worse (but, I fear, more common), the preacher's own personal anger. Focusing the conflict keeps it alive until an appropriate resolution can occur. It maintains the tension needed for discovery, for creative appropriation of what the conflict means, for the level of personal investment we have to achieve if restoration is going to occur.

5. The focusing just spoken of goes on in part through what I would call *structuring and restructuring the conflict* linguistically to make it available to the consciousness of the people. We need to take some care here that the conflict is structured for accessability at all levels of our functioning—cognitive, emotional, and behavioral. What the conflict consists of and means, what feelings it involves, and what actions it spawns become the content of the structuring process.

6. Our final task is to *provide interpretative tools,* largely through symbols and concepts, so that our people can wage the conflict in whose dynamics they are caught up. If focusing the conflict is what we mean by prophetic preaching, providing interpretative tools should be what we mean by the traditional corresponding concept, "priestly" preaching. The priestly function is not solving people's conflicts for them, still less engineering clever escapes into false peacefulness, but rather helping them discover the means whereby they may wage those conflicts successfully themselves. Much of what we have talked about in these pages as the interpretative role of theological language comes to roost here. When we have helped people learn a language through which they can engage, resolve, and reengage conflict at a higher level, then we have given them the tools they need—tools for restoration.

9. Endnote: "The City of Sadness," A Sermon

Whether to include any sermon in this book has caused me a mild vexation for several months; whether to include one of my *own* has occasioned real terror. I finally do so not because I want to offer a model, God forbid, of anything, but simply because if you as a reader have stayed with me through these pages we have formed a bond of sorts and I owe you at least this much of putting my money where my mouth is. Whenever I hold out any of my own *praxis* for inspection, I call to mind, at least inwardly, the example of this century's greatest teacher of piano composition, Lydia Boulanger, who taught the best of them—but could play little herself.

This sermon is flawed in several important ways, length among them. But it does embody, I believe, the major concerns of the preceding chapters, and I want to offer it as a minor case study of what I have been talking about. It does try to represent that marriage of biblical-theological witness with pastoral concern that I have written about in these pages. This sermon would fall into the third category I wrote about in the first chapter: it tries to address a specific pastoral issue quite directly. As for "proclamation," perhaps it needs a touch more—but only a touch. The field it tries to claim is the first I wrote about, the symbolic one, which is, frankly, where I myself am most comfortable. Since it has a great deal of my immediate personal history in its background, it will illustrate, positively or negatively, the whole matter of using oneself in preaching. As to the context for restoration, the subject matter itself comes to my rescue: I am trying to talk about liminality and the *communitas* bond of marginal people. And the issues of the sermon? Perhaps all four I mentioned are there; you will have to decide how faithfully I took my own advice.

THE CITY OF SADNESS

By the waters of Babylon, there we sat down and wept,
    when we remembered Zion.
On the willows there we hung up our lyres.
For there our captors required of us songs,
and our tormentors, mirth, saying,
    "Sing us one of the songs of Zion!"
How shall we sing the Lord's song in a foreign land?
If I forget you, O Jerusalem,
    let my right hand wither!
Let my tongue cleave to the roof of my mouth,
    if I do not remember you,
    if I do not set Jerusalem
    above my highest joy!

Psalm 137:1–6

Now faith is the assurance of things hoped for, the conviction of things not seen. . . . These [Old Testament exiles] all died in faith, not having received what was promised, but having seen it and greeted it from afar, and having acknowledged that they were strangers and exiles on the earth.

For people who speak in this way about themselves make it plain that they are in search of their real homeland. They can hardly have meant the country they came from, since they had the opportunity to go back to it; but in fact they were longing for a better homeland, their heavenly homeland. That is why God is not ashamed to be called their God, for he has prepared for them a city.

Hebrews 11:1, 13–16

Then I saw a new heaven and a new earth; the first heaven and the first earth had disappeared now, and there was no longer any sea. I saw the holy city, and the New Jerusalem, coming down from God out of heaven, as beautiful as a bride all dressed for her husband.

Then I heard a loud voice call from the throne, "You see this city? Here God lives among his people. He will make his home among them; they shall be his people, and he will be their God; his name is God-with-them. He will wipe away all tears from their eyes; there will be no more death, and no more mourning or sadness. The world of the past has gone.

Revelation 21:2–4

This will not be an easy sermon, either for me to preach or for you to hear. I make no promises, except that each of us will in his or her own way find the subject of sadness familiar. If, at the end, the truth about ourselves, and about God, has been canted to a slightly more accessible angle than it was before, that will be enough.

We do not know much, any more, about sadness. Even the feeling itself is more a stranger than it used to be, not because there is so little of it but because it has lost its clearness, its line and form. Sadness has taken too many partners—depression, frustration, disappointment, and more—for us to know it well on its own, and in that we have lost something, which we might do well to find again.

Here is the ending I am reaching for: a sense that sadness—unalloyed, annealed by life on its own terms—can be a form of love. Someone said that the primeval creative sound is that of a great transcendent heart breaking. You can call it the love of God if you wish, but whatever you call it, it will never leave you alone, and to know that love and to live in the city it builds and beckons us to comes at least in part from sadness.

"City" may seem at first an odd metaphor to use. It is, admittedly, a holdover from those ancient Old Testament writers whose nomadism made them look upon something as secure and settled as a city as one of creation's greatest gifts. Christianity, even in its urbanization, never quite lost its fascination with the idea. It acquired overtones of something beyond what we could point to in the here-and-now, a time of rest and settlement, and as the writer of *Revelation* develops it, the final symbol for the end of travail and the culmination of eternity. And so, for our purposes, the gossamer threads of sadness weave a tapestry whose design is a city.

We Americans are increasingly aware of the state of our mental health, and we use with ease terminology that once was reserved to the mysterious vocabulary of the psychotherapist. Any good bookstore will serve you a selection of titles with words like "depression" or "neurosis" or "mourning" or "aggression" in them, and on the whole most of you would know what they mean. It is a great gain for psychological counseling in its various forms to have come out from under the wraps of secrecy and shamefulness, and I would not have it any other way. I sometimes marvel at the basic knowledge of emotional processes now that was simply a mystery to most people a generation ago.

But, at the same time, we have paid a price for our knowledge, and I am afraid it may be this: that sometimes we get so tangled up in our newfound vocabulary as to lose touch with some fundamental experiences and so overly complicate ourselves. Sadness is one of them. Let me give you a small example of my own. I am, as some of you know, a practicing psychotherapist as well as a clergyman, and as most such people do from time to time, I go for professional help when the going gets rougher about something than I can ride through alone without getting thrown. Not long ago, finding myself in that spot, I consulted with a therapist for a short time. I thought of myself, in those particular circumstances, as rather frustrated and depressed, the result of being in a situation where I was momentarily helpless and beset by some unresolved conflicts of the past.

My therapist, however, used no such words. One day he simply commented, "The thing I have noticed over the last few weeks, Dr. Nichols, is that you are very sad." Not depressed, or bound up in anxiety, or caught by any of the baffling hybrids of feeling that proliferate so rapidly we can scarcely invent names fast enough for them. No, none of that: just sad. My first reaction was mildly shocked disbelief. Surely two well-qualified professionals, now in the roles of client and therapist, can come up with something more accurately complicated than that, I thought.

As time went by, however, I began to see the simple wisdom of it. Yes, my life situation was at that time complicated; and yes, I was ensnared by a web of different feelings, most of them unpleasant; and yes, too, I would have to "work through" all that, as we say, in order to come out on the other side. But those were the complex overtones of a struck piano wire. The fundamental tone that was being sounded was sadness, and it could not be subdivided further.

The relief of realizing that was quite amazing, rather like discovering that what I thought was a lost and twisted track in the wilderness was in fact a clear and well-marked, though terribly difficult, road. What I had to do was walk it. My companion would be sadness, and toward its city at the end of my road I would have to move. Only then, you see, could I catch the trailing edge of a suspicion that I was not alone, and that this might be a form of love.

This is not the time or place for personal confession. But what I must say is that my sadness is no longer an enemy. No, of course I do not like it. No one likes to be sad, except perhaps in those comparatively rare moments for most of us (and trag-ically common ones for some few) when sadness is embraced as one's only friend. But on the whole, that is not it. It is the sense that sadness will not be my undoing, even when it is all I have for the time being. You will have to look for yourselves at those private images of your own inner sanctuaries to know what that is like for you. For me, it is many things.

Sadness is watching my children at the threshold of learning more about the world than I secretly hoped they would ever have to know, and knowing for my part that there is no way under heaven I can protect them from the pain and disappoint-ment that will have to come to them. Far from it! Were I able to spare them that, I would take away what I now come to think of as their own right to sadness, and knowing that enriches, however dubiously and paradoxically, the same gift that be-longs to me.

Sadness is the memory of what I called a rare wild bird, and the straining of eyes to catch once more a fleeting glance of her heartbreaking beauty. It is the cold double ribbon of steel that unfurls itself behind a departing train and its precious cargo, or the earthbound silence of an airplane whose sound you can no longer hear as it takes away what you would give your life to have forever.

And mind you, sadness is not always quiet and forlorn. It can rage, and it can laugh; it can scream in the face of God, and it can dizzy itself in distraction. But when it is there, in whatever form, you know that the only thing that keeps your life together, second by second, is whatever it is beyond your sphere of consciousness that gives the sadness and keeps you from being overwhelmed. Perhaps that is what we mean by knowing the love of God: to be utterly, unspeakably in the darkness, but to sense, beyond any power of articulation or vision just now, that behind it is the light of life. That is the City of Sadness toward which we move.

How can one find anything of God in that? some will ask. How under heaven, if God's intention is grace and love, can we associate it with sadness? I am not trying to trick you or play those games with words that religious people have sometimes done to convince themselves that black is really white or that the world is somehow not what anyone's senses will plainly say it is. No, when you are sad and hear someone talk in this way, you have a right to ask some questions. Have we been misled? Is the love of God such a wrathful deceit after all? When our prayers or sighs call night and day for some relief from this torment, and when we cannot let ourselves suspect even for an instant that nothing more than our imaginations is at the other end of them because to do so would crush out the last hope of coming back into even the feeblest sunlight, how can we let ourselves believe that sadness might be God's aim—or worse, his weakness?

I know no answer that does not come back to the search for images. As Albert Camus said, "A man's work is nothing but this slow trek to rediscover, through the detours of art, those two or three great and simple images in whose presence his heart first opened."[1] And the image that comes to me is that I am bound up in the arms of a God who weeps but will not leave me alone even when his own heart is breaking. No, I do not understand it—neither has anyone who ever encountered it, so far as I can tell. I do not know how a young woman could look back on the hell of her own madness and remember that what kept her alive, crazy as she was, was saying over and over again, "God, you've abandoned me for now and I don't know why you hate me, *but I won't turn loose of you.*" I do not know how Paul believed that power is made perfect in weakness, any more than I know how that phantasm of John the Divine could see beyond the barbarism and persecution of Rome to a city where there would be no more tears and no more sadness. But somehow, like coming upon the skyline of New York at dusk, despite the earthworm trails you had no choice but to follow to get there, somehow love is there, in the City of Sadness. And one comes to sense that it is the same love that was "caught up in the wind like a scrap of paper and placarded against a cross" and endures—holding, weeping, beating forever.[2]

Do not let me or anyone else mislead you: none of this gives easy comfort or quickly takes the pain away. What it does, instead, is remind us that what we thought was the end of any reason for caring a damn about the next tick of the clock turns out to be some kind of a beginning—in mystery and confusion, with the ground fog rising and falling around your feet, the beginning of a journey. To take it means we have to get closer to our sadness, even when all our instincts vote to put as much distance on it as we can.

Sadness can be an empty feeling, paralyzing will and desire. It can so magnetize your thinking that you find yourself drawn again and again to the very thing that makes you sad. It will not let you get away from it, and the last thing that helps is the effort of friends to "take your mind off it," as they say. How in God's name can you take your mind off something that has completely captured it and will not let it go? Those are the times you find it hard to do anything at all with yourself, and familiar pleasures, even passions, are as cold as winter ashes to you.

But, strange to say, sadness can be a giving feeling too. Sometimes it starts us reaching for what we never knew was priceless until tears washed away the layers of pretense and avoidance and left it shining and beckoning. Sadness can make you yearn and in your yearning turn to what may someday bring its fulfillment—no matter that just now you can't say how. I have searched each passerby hunting for the beautiful face I had loved and lost, knowing it was just not there to be found any more, but knowing too that learning to love again was now my task and my heart's desire. I have left places of worship in the grip of unspeakable sadness because what had happened there so insulted my spirit and betrayed my need, only to discover that that feeling made clearer than ever before how much I wanted to be in the presence of God. In that was a recommitment of sorts, born of deprivation, yes, but dedicated once again to finding what would give it sustenance. Some of the most beautiful music I ever heard was the chanting of Greek peasant women, tears streaming down their lined and hardened faces, in a church on Corfu one Good Friday evening. I asked someone who knew better than I why they were weeping. "Because," he said, "their Christ is dead." I have often thought that I will never understand what resurrection means until I can weep like that. Sadness, you see, can, in its own unpredictable and maddening way, teach you to love again.

There is another thing about sadness that we mustn't forget: it isn't all the same. Sometimes it is a grinding ache so deep in your body you know it has to be the soul. But sometimes it is not an ache at all, and that is what we mean, I think, when we speak of "weeping for joy." I do not mean those moments when impossible tension breaks and floods out in tears of relief. No, I mean real weeping, real sadness, but the kind that carries with it something like gratitude, perhaps, or hope.

It is the sort of feeling you have on discovering that something or someone you thought was lost is safe after all, even though now it lies forever beyond your reach. It is seeing the escape from danger of what you feared would perish, while at the same time you realize it must now live safely in a world you do not inhabit, much as you want to. You rejoice and you weep, and what we sometimes are foolishly taught to believe are contrary feelings embrace each other in what I suppose is one of the most baffling and heartbreaking and awe-inspiring sort of moments a person can have. It is almost indescribable, like putting into words the color of a mourning dove, or recapturing the scent of wild honeysuckle from a country road in summer. It is all there and all yours, but you know you don't own it and never will.

The mysteriousness of that sadness, though, is what makes it so important, and the closest I can come to understanding it is to believe that "weeping for joy" is a time when the human spirit transcends itself, setting aside its own agenda even for only an instant. If we are given anything like communion with creation, then that must be what it is like. I have seen it, sometimes, on the faces of the dying, and I have felt myself in its grip witnessing the moment of birth. Theologians are not very well equipped to talk about it; poets and artists do far better. I used to listen to Robert Frost "say" his poems in his last years, and it was there, always there in that dying old man's artless elegance. It constitutes an invitation to that venture of the spirit that Christopher Fry extends in the setting of war's grime and fear:

> Dark and cold we may be, but this
> Is no winter now. The frozen misery
> Of centuries breaks, cracks, begins to move,
> The thunder is the thunder of the floes,
> The thaw, the flood, the upstart spring.
> Thank God our time is now when wrong
> Comes up to face us everywhere,
> Never to leave us till we take
> The longest stride of soul men ever took.
> Affairs are now soul-size.
> The enterprise
> Is exploration into God.[3]

All I am saying is that your sadness is not a single hue, an unwavering tone, any more than love is. It is not always a "problem to be solved" or a "burden to be borne"; sometimes it is a life to be lived, and if there are not enough colors on its palette to paint in all the pleasures of the daylight, then there are surely enough for whatever it is that is worth one's living and dying for.

Let me change direction now. Sometimes sadness does more than get us outside ourselves; it can also tell us some things about ourselves we might never have noticed before. It teaches painfully but well about our wants, our fears, our values. It is more than whistling in the dark to say that sometimes what life means for you is never so transparently clear as when what gives that meaning slips out of your grasp, and you are sad. Let me try to tell you one way that works, because I think you will recognize it.

Sadness is not always a feeling; sometimes it is just the situation of our lives, a stage set we have wandered onto, wondering what our lines are supposed to be. Then is when we are apt to say things like "It is so sad what has happened" or "The poor fellow is caught in such sad straits." Then is when sometimes the very drama we are caught in, irrespective of what we feel inside, acts out for us the paradigm of our own internal vision for us to see as though it were being shown us in a picture.

"Insight," we sometimes call it, "the moment of truth," "the time of reckoning"—no matter: it is when sadness leaves as its paradoxical gift a new awareness of what we, deep inside ourselves, are truly like. And sometimes what we receive together with that gift is the power to go on, somehow, into what was unopened territory before. That isn't easy to grasp, I know. But here is how I have seen it work. A young man I know has labored through a depressing series of collapsed business ventures, beautiful dreams gone blighted by heaven knows what misfortunes—brilliant ideas followed by dismal failures, each of them adding its weight of heartsickness.

A sad situation, we would say, and rightly so. That is the point. Except that one day for this man "the penny dropped," and the sadness of his situation showed him something about himself he had never seen before: that deep inside he possessed a fatal attraction to dreams that in the cold daylight of reality would not work—rather like the man who having lost yet another love comes to realize through the sadness of it that he is addicted to hidden and elusive women. I do not say for a moment that it makes the pain any less; but for some of us, some of the time, it can be a "message in a bottle," as Walker Percy says, and on a good day we had no right predicting, it may just save us.[4]

The Bible, by the way, almost never speaks of sadness, except in a rather passing way. But you cannot read the Bible long without discovering that sadness lives on nearly every page. Nowhere is it more pronounced than when those men and women of doubt and faith, over a span of two thousand years, stared into their feeble little campfires in the wilderness or huddled together in the treacherous shade of Roman arches and saw that they were, in the end, strangers and exiles on the earth. If there is one theme in biblical faith that you can't avoid in even the most passing acquaintance, that is it.

In fact, so strong is the song of the exile—the expatriate, we would say in modern terms—in all of human history that I doubt anything comes quite so close to the inner strivings of the human soul as it measures out its days, here in little increments of finite misery, and there in great swathes of eternity. "These all died in faith," says the writer to the Hebrews, "not having received what was promised, but having seen it and greeted it from afar, and acknowledged that they were strangers and exiles on the earth. That is why God is not ashamed to be called their God, since he has founded the City for them."

That, I think, is perhaps the Bible's ultimate description of the posture of faith, and there is no word to describe it but sadness. Notice, though, that there is one expatriatism of fear and another of hope. There is fleeing from Sodom and Gomorrah, and there is the slow walk back from Jerusalem to Emmaus late that Sunday afternoon. When you read the literature of expatriate writers, you sense the difference at once between those who are so desperately frightened that what once lived inside them has withered and died and those who search still for a promise once received and never quite abandoned, no matter how damning the evidence. The first is despair, and there is no life in it; the other is sadness, and when it is clearest, it can be the heartbeat of life and hope.

You can be a stranger and an exile without ever leaving Main Street, or Central Park West, or Yazoo, Mississippi (as Willie Morris would say).[5] You can be one when you have had a taste of glory and then the ache of hunger for what you couldn't reach again, when you have felt your spirit soar with the promise of what you never thought could be only then to elude you while laying its vapor trail across the horizon of your dreams. And for all of us there will be times when we kick the red dirt that sticks in our throats and wallow in our dung heaps of rejection and curse the terrors of the night; but the gift of it, the real thing, melted down and owing nothing to anybody, is that we will have seen it and greeted it from afar and continued to lurch our way toward a City of Sadness in which, beyond our power to ask or imagine, there is no mourning.

That is what being a stranger and an exile means, and I do not know whether anyone has ever reached for the love of their lives, whatever or whomever it may be, without inheriting that mantle. I want to say that something shifts deep inside the human soul when we stop trying to escape that meaning, and embrace it instead, no matter that our hands shake and our eyes "cry down tears." No, it will not be pleasant, and nothing of giddiness lies in that feeling. But the sadness marks a pathway, and even hating every step of the way, the exile walks it toward what shimmers afar off as the city prepared in love for such as we. Do not scorn the expatriate as a lost one; he or she is what Jesus once called a "little one," for whom much is prepared and everything given.

Yes, I am saying that more of us are strangers and exiles than we may once have thought, and perhaps that is the point I have been straining for all this time. We have worried for years about the loss of cultural rootage in this country, about the alienation of the young (and now not-so-young) from a sense of their history and value, about the collapse of the family's molecular structure and the resulting fragmentation and trivialization of relationships. What we haven't always recognized, however, is that exile is rooted in the human experience far too deeply to think about "curing" or "solving," least of all with the sort of religious anesthesia you get these days about recapturing lost days of stability and faith.

Recapture what, for God's sake? Ruth leaving her homeland? David weeping into the wreckage of his life, "Absalom, Absalom"? The waters of Babylon? The whole anguished cry of the New Testament that echoes from Golgotha to Patmos, "Maranatha, even now Lord Jesus, come"? If we were honest, what we would recapture is the sadness of the pilgrim, and at the same time the presence of the God who mourns our flinging away to false assurances as surely as we wonder how we shall ever "sing the Lord's song in a foreign land."

Frederick Buechner writes of that from the vantage point of his own boyhood sadness:

A crazy, holy grace I have called it. Crazy because whoever could have predicted it? Who can ever foresee the crazy how and when and where of a grace that wells up out of the lostness and pain of the world and of our own inner worlds? And holy because these moments of grace come ultimately from farther away than Oz and deeper down than doom, holy because they heal and hallow. "For all thy blessings, known and unknown, remembered and forgotten, we give thee thanks," runs an old prayer, and it is for the all but unknown ones and the more than half forgotten ones that we do well to look back over the journeys of our lives, because it is their presence that makes the life of each of us a sacred journey. We have a hard time seeing such blessed and blessing moments as the gifts I choose to believe they are, and a harder time still reaching out toward the hope of a giving hand, but part of the gift is to be able, at least from time to time, to be assured and convinced without seeing, as Hebrews says, because that is of the very style and substance of faith as well as what drives it always to seek a farther and a deeper seeing still. . . . Faith in something—if only in the proposition that life is better than death—is what makes our journeys through time bearable.[6]

We have come to the end. All I am trying to say is that while we know that sadness may try our faith unmercifully, we would also do well to wonder whether sadness may also, in its mysterious way, bestow a blessing of love. And if that is even remotely true, then I say, do not put down your sadness until it has given its gift to you; and even in the tearful cursing of your fortunes that you have a perfect right to do, do not trade your lot for the nearest respite, lest you miss its crazy, holy grace.

We keep picking our way through the rocks and brambles of our days, toward what we see from afar as a City of Sadness, because the voice of the exile sings of no more crying there. In mystery and in promise, it is prepared for us.

Notes

Introduction

1. Robert Lindner, *The Fifty-Minute Hour* (New York: Holt, Rinehart & Winston, 1955), p. 205.
2. Ibid., p. 207.
3. Karl Barth, *The Word of God and the Word of Man*, trans. Douglas Horton (Boston: Pilgrim Press, 1928), pp. 107–08.

Chapter 2

1. J. Randall Nichols, *Building the Word: The Dynamics of Communication and Preaching* (San Francisco: Harper & Row, 1980).
2. Frederick Buechner, *The Sacred Journey* (San Francisco: Harper & Row, 1982).
3. Ian T. Ramsey, *Religious Language: An Empirical Placing of Theological Phrases* (New York: Macmillan Co., 1957).
4. Nichols, *Building the Word*, pp. 66–68.
5. Laurence H. Stookey, "Critique: A Sermon Subverted," *Homiletic* 7, no. 2: (1982) pp. 1–5.
6. Martin E. P. Seligman, *Helplessness: On Depression, Development, and Death* (San Francisco: W. H. Freeman & Co., 1975).
7. William Muehl, *All the Damned Angels* (Philadelphia: United Church Press, 1972), pp. 33–39.
8. Granger E. Westberg, *Good Grief* (Philadelphia: Fortress Press, 1962).
9. Clement Welsh, *Preaching in a New Key: Studies in the Psychology of Thinking and Listening* (Philadelphia: United Church Press, 1974).

Chapter 3

1. Edward T. Hall, *The Silent Language* (New York: Doubleday & Co., 1959).
2. Diogenes Allen, *The Reasonableness of Faith: A Philosophical Essay on the Grounds for Religious Beliefs* (Washington, D.C.: Corpus Books, 1968), p. 4.
3. Ramsey, *Religious Language*.
4. Janet Malcolm, *Psychoanalysis: The Impossible Profession* (New York: Alfred A. Knopf, 1981).
5. Paul Ricoeur, "Biblical Hermeneutics," *Semeia* 4 (1975): p. 78.
6. Stephen Crites, "The Narrative Quality of Experience," *Journal of the American Academy of Religion* 39, no. 3 (September 1971).
7. Thor Hall, *The Future Shape of Preaching* (Philadelphia: Fortress Press, 1971), p. 4.
8. Shirley G. Guthrie, Jr., "The Narcissism of American Piety: The Disease and the Cure," *Journal of Pastoral Care* 21, no. 4 (December 1977): pp. 220–29.

Chapter 4

1. Harry Emerson Fosdick, *The Living of These Days: An Autobiography* (New York: Harper & Row, 1956), p. 94.
2. D. W. Winnicott, *Through Paediatrics to Psychoanalysis* (New York: Basic Books, 1975); Simon A. Grolnick, ed., *Between Reality and Fantasy: Transitional Objects and Phenomena* (New York: Jason Aronson, 1978).
3. Thomas C. Oden, *Kerygma and Counseling: Toward a Covenant Ontology for Secular Psychotherapy* (Philadelphia: Westminster Press, 1967), p. 26.

Chapter 5

1. Bruce D. Reed, *The Dynamics of Religion: Process and Movement in Christian Churches* (London: Darton, Longman & Todd), pp. 25–30.

2. Robert Langs, "Some Communicative Properties of the Bipersonal Field," in *Technique in Transition* (New York: Jason Aronson, 1978), pp. 413–71.

3. Ricoeur, "Biblical Hermeneutics," p. 78.

4. Langs, "Some Communicative Properties," p. 437.

5. Ibid., pp. 443–44.

Chapter 6

1. Phillips Brooks, *On Preaching* (New York: Seabury Press, 1964).

2. H. H. Farmer, *The Servant of the Word* (New York: Charles Scribner's Sons, 1942); Edmund Holt Linn, *Preaching as Counseling: The Unique Method of Harry Emerson Fosdick* (Valley Forge, Pa.: Judson Press, 1966); John Oman, *Concerning the Ministry* (London: SCM Press, 1936); Reuel L. Howe, *Partners in Preaching: Clergy and Laity in Dialogue* (New York: Seabury Press, 1967).

3. Donald P. Spence, *Narrative Truth and Historical Truth: Meaning and Interpretation in Psychoanalysis* (New York: W. W. Norton & Co., 1982).

4. Paul Watzlawick, ed., *The Invented Reality: How Do We Know What We Believe We Know? Contributions to Constructionism* (New York: W. W. Norton & Co., 1984).

5. Frederick Buechner, *Now and Then* (New York: Harper & Row, 1983) and *The Sacred Journey;* Russell Baker, *Growing Up* (New York: St. Martin's Press, 1982).

6. Carl R. Rogers, *On Becoming a Person: A Therapist's View of Psychotherapy* (Boston: Houghton Mifflin Co., 1961).

7. Ibid., p. 50.

8. Ibid., p. 51.

9. Ibid., p. 52.

10. Ibid., p. 52.

11. Ibid., p. 53.

12. Ibid., p. 53.

13. Ibid., p. 54.

14. Guthrie, "Narcissism of American Piety."

15. Rogers, *On Becoming a Person,* p. 54.

16. Seward Hiltner, "The Minister in the Human Circus," *Pastoral Psychology* (December 1971): pp. 13–20.

17. Rogers, *On Becoming a Person,* p. 54.

18. Ibid., p. 55.

Chapter 7

1. Harry Emerson Fosdick, *The Meaning of Prayer* (Follet Publishing Co., 1949), p. 143.

2. A portion of this section first appeared as "Worship As Anti-Structure: The Contribution of Victor Turner," *Theology Today* 41, no. 4 (January 1985): pp. 401–09.

3. Victor Turner, *The Ritual Process* (Ithaca, N.Y.: Cornell University Press, 1969), p. 96.

4. Victor Turner, "Passages, Margins, and Poverty: Religious Symbols of Communitas," *Worship* 46, nos. 7 and 8, (August–September 1972): p. 393.

5. Turner, "Passages," p. 400.

6. Turner, *The Ritual Process,* pp. 106–7.

7. Ibid., p. 97.

8. Ibid., p. 129.

9. Michael Novak, *Ascent of the Mountain, Flight of the Dove: An Invitation To Religious Studies* (New York: Harper & Row, 1971).

10. Turner, *The Ritual Process*, p. 129.

11. Turner, "Passages," p. 399.

12. Ibid., p. 409.

13. Ibid., p. 494.

14. Ibid., p. 391.

15. Ibid., pp. 486–87.

16. Martin Buber, *Between man and man*, Trans. R. G. Smith, (London: Fontana Library, 1961), p. 51, quoted in Turner, *The Ritual Process*, p. 127.

17. Turner, "Passages," pp. 492–3.

18. See, for instance, Harold Garfinkle, *Studies in Ethnomethodology* (Englewood Cliffs, N.J.: Prentice-Hall, 1967).

19. Paul W. Pruyser, *The Minister as Diagnostician: Personal Problems in Pastoral Perspective* (Philadelphia: Westminster Press, 1976), pp. 60–79.

20. Erik H. Erikson, *Insight and Responsibility: Lectures on the Ethical Implications of Psychoanalytic Insight* (New York: W. W. Norton & Co., 1964).

Chapter 8

1. Roy W. Fairchild, *Finding Hope Again: A Pastor's Guide to Counseling Depressed Persons* (New York: Harper & Row, 1980).

2. Ibid., pp. 15–16.

3. Seligman, *Helplessness*.

4. Hiltner, "The Minister in the Human Circus," p. 19.

5. Lewis R. Rambo, *The Divorcing Christian* (Nashville: Abingdon Press, 1983).

6. Robert E. Buxbaum, personal conversation, San Antonio, Texas, May 1985.

7. Bernard Steinzor, *When Parents Divorce: A New Approach to New Relationships* (New York: Pantheon Books, 1969).

8. James N. Lapsley, "Reconciliation, Forgiveness, Lost Contracts," *Theology Today* 23, no. 1 (April 1966).

9. Elisabeth Kubler-Ross, ed., *Death: The Final Stage of Growth* (Englewood Cliffs, N.J.: Prentice-Hall, 1983).

10. Eric Lindemann, "Symptomatology and Management of Acute Grief," *American Journal of Psychiatry* 101 (1944):141–9.

11. John Bowlby, *Attachment and Loss* (New York: Basic Books, 1969–1980), 3: *Loss, Sadness, and Depression*, p. 85.

12. Edmund Morris, *The Rise of Theodore Roosevelt* (New York: Coward, McCann & Geoheagan, 1979), p. 244.

13. Linn, *Preaching as Counseling*.

14. Bowlby, *Attachment and Loss*, vol. 1, *Attachment;* vol. 2, *Separation: Anxiety and Anger;* vol. 3, *Loss, Sadness, and Depression*.

15. Robert Jay Lifton, *The Life of the Self: Toward a New Psychology* (New York: Simon & Schuster, 1976), p. 37. See also Lifton, *The Broken Connection: On Death and the Continuity of Life* (New York: Simon & Schuster, 1979).

16. Seligman, *Helplessness*, pp. 176–81.

17. Lifton, *The Life of the Self*, p. 39.

18. Ulrich Simon, *Theology of Crisis* (London: SPCK, 1948).

Chapter 9
1. Albert Camus, 1958 preface to *The Wrong Side and the Right Side* (n.p.).
2. Paul Scherer, "When God Isn't Around," sermon preached in the chapel of Princeton University, Princeton, New Jersey, May 2, 1965. Personal recording.
3. Christopher Fry, *A Sleep of Prisoners* (New York: Oxford University Press, 1951).
4. Walker Percy, *The Message in the Bottle: How Queer Man Is, How Queer Language Is, and What One Has to Do with the Other* (New York: Farrar, Strauss & Giroux, 1975).
5. Willie Morris, *North Toward Home* (New York: Delta Books, 1970).
6. Frederick Buechner, *The Sacred Journey*, pp. 57–58.

Index

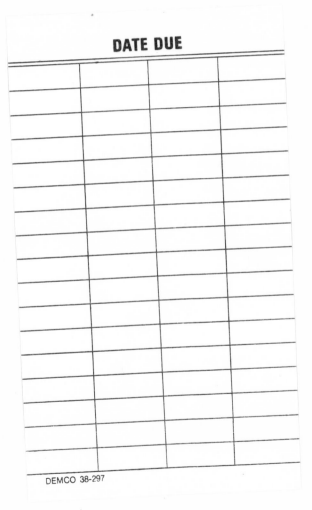